Connecting and Communicating
with Your Autistic Child

of related interest

**Building Communication and Independence for
Children Across the Autism Spectrum**
Strategies to Address Minimal Language, Echolalia and Behavior
Elizabeth Ives Field
ISBN 978 1 78775 546 8
eISBN 978 1 78775 547 5

Having Fun with Feelings on the Autism Spectrum
The CBT Activity Book for Kids Age 4–8
*Michelle Garnett, Tony Attwood, Louise Ford,
Stefanie Runham and Julia Cook*
ISBN 978 1 78775 327 3
eISBN 978 1 78775 328 0

10 Steps to Reducing Your Child's Anxiety on the Autism Spectrum
The CBT-Based 'Fun With Feelings' Parent Manual
*Michelle Garnett, Tony Attwood, Louise Ford,
Stefanie Runham and Julia Cook*
ISBN 978 1 78775 325 9
eISBN 978 1 78775 326 6

**The Autism Discussion Page on Stress,
Anxiety, Shutdowns and Meltdowns**
Proactive Strategies for Minimizing Sensory, Social and Emotional Overload
Bill Nason
ISBN 978 1 78592 804 8
eISBN 978 1 78450 834 0

Connecting and Communicating with Your Autistic Child

A Toolkit of Activities to Encourage Emotional
Regulation and Social Development

Act for Autism

Foreword by Glenys Jones,
CPsychol, AfBPS, MA

Jessica Kingsley Publishers
London and Philadelphia

First published in Great Britain in 2021 by Jessica Kingsley Publishers
An Hachette Company

1

Copyright © Jane Gurnett and Tessa Morton 2021
Foreword copyright © Glenys Jones 2021

Illustrations are by Lynn Redwood and have been reproduced with permission.

Phoebe Caldwell's quote is reproduced from *The Anger Box* (2014),
with the permission of Pavilion Publishing and Media.

Quotes from Fletcher-Watson, S. and Happé, F. (2019) *Autism: A New
Introduction to Psychological Theory and Current Debate*. Abingdon: Routledge
are reproduced with permission of the Licensor through PLSclear.

Quote from Reynolds, D. and Reason, M. (2012) *Kinesthetic
Empathy in Creative and Cultural Practices*. Bristol: Intellect Ltd is
reproduced with permission of the Licensor through PLSclear.

Front cover image source: Lynn Redwood.

A CIP catalogue record for this title is available from the
British Library and the Library of Congress

ISBN 978 1 78775 550 5
eISBN 978 1 78775 551 2

Printed and bound by CPI Group (UK) Ltd, Croydon, CR0 4YY

Jessica Kingsley Publishers' policy is to use papers that are natural,
renewable and recyclable products and made from wood grown in
sustainable forests. The logging and manufacturing processes are expected
to conform to the environmental regulations of the country of origin.

Jessica Kingsley Publishers
Carmelite House
50 Victoria Embankment
London EC4Y 0DZ

www.jkp.com

Dedicated to Barney and Rosa

*'Many children are daffodils, consistent and
predictable. Our children are orchids. Orchids
have a mystique that seems to set them apart from
most other flowers; it takes nurture and patience
for them to reach full bloom.' (Act for Autism)*

Contents

Foreword

Over the last 40 years in the field of autism and education, there has been a growing literature on approaches developed to support parents and professionals alike. Some approaches have focused on developing particular skills for working directly with the child or young person. Other approaches have focused on encouraging professionals and parents to adapt their style and communication in order to build a positive and trusting relationship as a foundation for social understanding and effective communication. This book sits in the latter category. There are key messages within it on how best to engage, relate to and communicate with autistic children, young people and adults alike.

Many ideas that underpin the book have come directly from conversations with autistic children and young people, and adult autobiographies. These accounts give great insights into the sensory and social challenges that can occur. In particular, autistic children and adults often have strong adverse reactions to brightly lit, noisy, crowded environments. They often say they are expected to operate in a world that has not been designed for autism, and that as they grow older, people assume they will have learned how to do so. But it is clear from their life stories that many challenges they experience as children remain as adults. What changes, for some, is that they learn to understand what these challenges are, can communicate them to others, and either actively avoid or manage them. This book aims to help in this process by making others aware of some of the issues and suggesting ways for effective communication to be established. When a person can adapt their world to fit their profile and interests, they are likely to experience better physical and mental well-being.

The Act for Autism authors Tessa Morton and Jane Gurnett acknowledge the increased emphasis in the literature on the importance of attending to the physical and sensory environment and the actions, expectations and responses of others (e.g. parents, family members and professionals). They point out that this needs to be individualized for each child and young person as every individual reacts differently. They argue that it is important also that the professional or parent has an understanding of how autism might influence an individual's thinking and actions so that they can adjust and make appropriate decisions on how best to help the individual relax, feel comfortable, and regulate their emotions and reduce anxiety when they are very distressed and upset.

The book starts with a short biography explaining how the authors came to work together and how their ideas for the book were formed. A brief history of autism is given, followed by current understandings, with a focus on sensory processing. In the second part of the book, the authors explain their approach in helping others to understand how autism might feel – in their words, what it is like to 'walk in the shoes of the person with autism'. Their ideas have developed and evolved over time from their direct work with parent groups, staff in schools and children and young people. They set out in separate chapters the ways they believe are effective in promoting connection and communication – Clear Time and the 3C Pathway. Clear Time is a directive to adults to ensure that they are free of distractions when they are with the child using the 3C Pathway. The 3Cs stand for connecting, calming and communicating. For each C, there are several exercises designed to achieve connection, calm and communication. The authors have a background in drama, acting and teaching, so many of the techniques they have learned underpin these exercises and these are well tried and tested in their workshops.

For parents or professionals keen to establish and build on an effective relationship with the children, young people or adults they live or work with, this book has a wealth of ideas on how this might be achieved. It encourages a calm, distraction-free way of being that respects how the individual might be feeling or thinking and one where they are able to communicate this non-verbally or verbally. Freeing oneself of expectations is key as these can be perceived as a demand and therefore pressurizing. Although the book is written with autism in mind, it is likely that readers might also view the ideas put forward as a good way to relate to all children and young people – to give them quality time, to help them become and stay calm, and to avoid having expectations on what might be.

Dr Glenys Jones
Autism Centre for Education and Research
University of Birmingham

Acknowledgements

Our thanks to:

Poppy Whittaker for always showing such consideration and patience as a 'super' sibling.

Lynda Lowe for her amazing support and faith in the early days.

Alice, Pernille, Charlotte, Luca, Jordan, Nathanial, Jacob, George, Sam, Teddy, Andrew, Jenny, Maise, Louise, Rob, and all the past and present drama crew.

Joy Harrison for the dance routines and production expertise.

Sam Powers and his team for their encouragement and spirit of joy.

Olivia Horgan for her support.

Paula Hubbard and Anna Lawrence for their editing support.

Lynn Barton for encouraging us in our first tender.

School for Social Enterprises start-up programme, sponsored

by Lloyds Banking Group, for getting us to take business seriously.

Peter Bazeley at the Inclusive Leisure Education Activities Project for supporting us to run our drama club.

John Hassell who initiated our first workshop.

Julie Hampton, Julie Bates and Jane Young for their parent workshop facilitation.

Phoebe Caldwell for sharing her practice.

And Dr Glenys Jones for her wisdom, expertise, encouragement and advice.

Also, in alphabetical order:
Linda Allan, Angus Baskerville, Emma Bond, Simon Dainty, Tracey Evans, Louise Gold, Aleks John, Michelle John, Pippa Kitchen, Lorraine MacAlister, Patrick Robinson, Felicity Steel, Tim Whittaker, Kirsten Wittemeyer.

Introduction

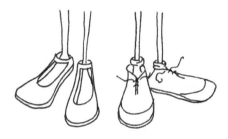

'To empathetically connect with someone you need to try and "walk in their shoes".'

(Act for Autism 2020)

How to make the best use of this book

Act for Autism is an award-winning not-for-profit social enterprise that provides training and support, founded by Tessa Morton and Jane Gurnett in 2016. This book is inspired by the broad range of experiences we have had in raising our children and working in the field of autism.

There are many books about autism. This book is primarily a practical guide and you can simply turn to the 3C Pathway and start to connect with your child through our relational approach and exercises. Some of you may have a good working knowledge of autism as a condition, but some of you may be opening this book having recently received a diagnosis for your loved one or someone you know or work with. Either way, we hope you will benefit from our approach.

However, we feel you will appreciate how to connect with your child at a deeper level if you familiarize yourself with the context of autism. Autism has a complicated history and even today there are many conflicting approaches and opinions regarding what autism actually is. This can be confusing when trying to help the person you want to understand and support. In our approach, we try to simplify the confusion by using a relational person-centred approach which relies on us changing our communication through empathetic connections, rather than trying to change the autistic person's mode of communication. We have found that this approach is the most successful for all concerned.

Please note that within the book, case study names have been anonymized, excluding quotes from Paul Isaacs, autism training consultant.

Chapter 1

Act for Autism

Who, What and Why?

'I believe that all children have the potential to be their best self if we lean in and connect empathetically.'

(Jane)

'If you empower a child to become self-aware and able to express themselves, you give them the greatest gift of all.'

(Tessa)

Tessa

Jane and I met on a day in school when we were both looking for my son. He had texted me to say he was having a panic attack in the toilets and wanted to come out but could not because he was scared someone would see him. The school had alerted me to the fact that he was not in class. I could feel my concern rising and could feel an even bigger concern from the school. I met Jane or Miss Gurnett, as I knew her, at reception and she told me she knew where he was and had told the school staff that she was dealing with it.

She took all the heat out of the situation and reassured me that he was safe. And he was safe because she 'had his back', he knew he would not be fussed, punished or judged by her. He eventually came out, and we drove home. It was not the only time that Jane became my son's safe person in a place where often he felt terrified, alone and confused.

I first encountered the word Asperger's when my son was diagnosed when he was four and it's been an interesting and enlightening journey.

This isn't his story, as he can tell that. This is the story of my journey, as his mum, to understand as much as I could about my son's Asperger's (now known as autism) and how I could help him. I soon realized that it was not going to be an easy task. There were so many conflicting opinions about cause, interventions and prognosis that I could never find the one answer I wanted. I realized, after a lot of trial and error, that there was never going to be one answer to the questions I had. I came to see that the answers lay with him and all the other wonderful young people I would meet on my journey.

I looked very closely at the challenges my son faced, and the other children I had met, and could see that the main challenge was not fully understanding the rules of social engagement that are taken for granted by so many. I also noticed that, when stressed, it was hard for them to regulate emotions and senses, but when calm, around people who they trusted, doing what they were interested in, there seemed to be little or no problem. Learning and interacting under pressure seemed to cause so much stress and confusion that they would give up. I wanted to do something about this for my son and the other children I was meeting, so I set up playgroups at our house where they could be together in a relaxed place, without judgement, and able to just do their own thing. The parents could also relax as their children were not singled out as different, and they could witness their children calmly playing and connecting in their own unique way. I was a drama teacher, coach and workshop leader, specializing in communication skills by profession, so I adapted everything I knew to support them.

I set up a local regular drama group to see whether the children would enjoy having a more directed play activity and whether it would help them build confidence in the areas where they were struggling. This group is still running, with some of the original members now going to university and volunteering as helpers and advocates. I met many parents through the drama group and witnessed how many were struggling to connect with their children and how the anxiety of thinking about the future was impacting on the family. I decided to train as a counsellor, so I could support the parents' understanding of autism and help them to manage their emotions around their children.

This led me to a counselling placement in a large school. Many of the children on my caseload struggled in school, not academically but socially. Some were being excluded and misunderstood. Many did not have a diagnosis but had similar challenges to my son, so I supported them with my personal knowledge of autism. I connected, I was calm and showed them the breathing techniques I used to help me calm myself. I then allowed them to communicate when and how they liked. It was this simple process that enabled me to learn about them from just being with them, and vice versa.

I also realized that the school was not equipped to support them as they had little or no understanding of autism from the child's perspective. From that point on, I knew that I needed to help these students and their teachers have a better connection. I also wanted to support the wider community to understand autism too.

We set up **Act for Autism** in 2016 as a not-for-profit community interest company to legitimize the work I was already doing. Jane and I partnered to bring energy and creativity to training parents, teachers and healthcare professionals in autism understanding. We continue to run drama groups, create film projects and deliver counselling to young people and their families.

The writing of this book has been at the request of many of those teachers, healthcare professionals and parents. They have found real benefit from the simple practice we introduced into our training that we call **Clear Time** and the **3C Pathway**.

I first discovered the principles we set out in Clear Time and the 3C Pathway when my son was having a meltdown. I had noticed that our family pet spaniel, Honey, calmly rested her head on his thigh when he was in distress, though he never let me near him. Not only did he allow Honey to touch him, but the noticeable reduction in his distress that there was because of her presence gave me an insight into what he needed – a presence with no anxiety, no distractions and no expectations. My son would have regular, extreme meltdowns when under pressure to transition from one thing to another. Getting him to school was often very challenging for him and distressing for me. Mornings were fuelled with my anxiety, 'Will he, won't he? Shall I wait, or shall I give up? Do we go to school or stay at home today? Shall I ring work now or will it be okay?'

His energy would rise, as mine did, and he would end up in a ball under the table in deep distress. I would rush in and try and smother the distress out of him, talking him down and holding him tight. Eventually, it would work but not without taking its toll on both our energies. One time, I sensed he was in deep distress but the phone call I was on meant there was a delay in going to him. When I eventually rushed in I saw our dog lying along his side, nudging into him. Her tail was beating a rhythm on the carpet and my son's hand was patting her. He was moaning quietly in time with the beat and his energy was slowly coming down. I watched with curiosity. After a few minutes, the dog slowly got up and left. My son got up too and calmly carried on doing what he had been doing, as if the storm had passed, and it was safe to come out. He didn't see me, but I had just witnessed Clear Time in action for the first time. I was amazed at how calm it all was and how the dog had made little fuss and interaction, and it was that which had had a massive positive effect on my son's ability to regulate.

So, I vowed to try it. The next time my son was struggling with his anxiety and heading for a meltdown, I took a deep breath out and against all my instincts to 'fix and fuss', I entered the room calmly and slowly. I went to him and sat close by, breathing slowly and quietly. I firmly rested my hand on his thigh, beating a slow heartbeat rhythm. I wasn't sure at first, so I kept just breathing out and keeping my self 'clear' and after about five minutes, he placed his hand on mine and I could feel his energy coming down and a sense that he was grounding himself. Once he was calm, I slowly moved my hand away. He managed to regulate himself and carry on doing what he was doing with little or no apparent communication with me. Well, I say little or no apparent communication but, in that moment, we both communicated everything we needed to.

Jane

Tessa and I met through her son's school. I was his drama teacher and later became his form tutor. I was aware of Tessa's son's diagnosis and had read his notes, but what struck me was his ability to embody a duck or a swan, gliding regally on top of the water, but underneath the water, I could see he was paddling for his life. He would appear in the mornings and I would try to decide whether he was able to stay in the class or needed to go to a safe space.

Sometimes, he would go missing, hiding in the toilets or the music room. Emails would start to fly around the school, and everybody would be 'looking for Barney'. This only added to his anxiety and helped to exacerbate his feelings of isolation and difference.

It was on one of these occasions that Tessa and I eventually met in person. I was immediately struck by how this dynamic woman was coping. She appeared to be managing her anxiety so well, but I could also see that she was frustrated with the drama that was constantly arising. It seemed that we shared an unspoken feeling that taking our anxiety out of the situation was what was helping.

I suppose I shouldn't commit this to print, but I gave Tessa my private mobile number, which was against school policy, but it was a moment when compassion kicked in and rules flew out of the window. Tessa and I started a simple system whereby if her son had a bad start to the day, Tessa would send me a short text putting me in the picture.

It was an extremely simple strategy and, when he eventually talked about school experiences, her son said that it was this that had meant he had felt seen. He was safe in the knowledge that I was aware of the paddling but didn't try to help or manage him. Practically, I didn't do much more than, for example, on a bad morning, give him a little signal that he could go and sit in his safe space.

Not having expectations of him meant that I wasn't about to heap pressure on top of his already sensorially overloaded brain and body. Fifteen minutes in his safe space helped him to de-escalate himself. Sometimes I would text Tessa to let her know he was in his safe space and then she could help him to rejoin his class by sending him a few simple emojis, affirmations or instructions.

I came to teaching later in life, having been an actress for many years. This was an advantage in many ways, as I had life experience and the confidence to instinctively implement things. As a new teacher, I was required to undertake personal development and decided to take a postgraduate degree in teaching Shakespeare experientially. It was through this course that I started to become fascinated by the power of the heartbeat rhythm in Shakespeare's verse and especially the influence it had on the autistic pupils in my classes.

A drama classroom is a noisy place, much of the time, and can be overwhelming. Pupils are asked to engage in unpredictable tasks and all the senses are awakened. This can be daunting if you live in a world where everything already feels magnified, and you feel dislocated from your peers. In all the classes where we worked on heartbeat verse rhythms, it was the autistic pupils who appeared to enjoy the execution of it most.

I am still not sure, and neither are researchers, why this may be, but one theory is that the heartbeat is predictable and structured and so makes the person feel safe. I also feel that when a baby is safe in the womb with their mother's heartbeat as a constant soundscape, this is perhaps the unconscious safe place that a child subliminally wants to return to.

This observation led me to experiment more and more with strategies that I hoped would help the autistic pupils with their self-confidence. It also started me on a journey of devouring books, articles, papers, podcasts, tweets, you name it, anything, that helped me understand how I could best serve these pupils.

I didn't read properly until I was ten years old, caught, I think, somewhere between a belief that I was stupid (having relentlessly been told this by teachers) and an awareness that there are many ways to access and process information. I decided that I didn't want to watch pupils go through the self-doubt and crippling fear that I had gone through because I was different. These are the main reasons I became so interested in trying to identify ways to connect with pupils who find it hard to access school. In school, issues occur when someone is challenged by the way in which they are being taught and this stands in the way of them fulfilling their full potential. It is imperative that these pupils are helped to feel connected to their learning. Anxiety also stands in the way of learning for many autistic pupils. This led me to create connected moments, which I would use before I tried to communicate my wants.

When a teacher says to a non-autistic pupil, 'Don't be silly, of course you can do it' or 'Calm down, we are going to get nowhere if you are this anxious, it's all going to be fine', this may comfort them or give them a bit of a push. If you say these things to an autistic pupil, with the best will in the world, it is not going to have the desired effect. I have talked to autistic pupils who are desperate to calm down, but their bodies won't let them. I have spoken to pupils who say, 'How do I know it's going to be fine? Everything always goes wrong.' They live a life of fear and anxiety – fearful that they are letting you down, anxious that this feeling of panic is going to last forever.

Subsequently, after I had embarked on a BPhil in autism, a counsellor at the school asked if I would like to meet someone with whom he thought I would be interested in working. That someone turned out to be Tessa. He was not aware of our previous connection. As we talked in more depth, it was obvious that Tessa and I were a good fit, as she also had a background in drama.

Initially, we set about creating a workshop for teachers about autism awareness that allowed them, through drama exercises, to 'walk in the shoes' of someone with processing differences.

We wanted the participants to really feel what it might be like to experience and live in a world where every day can be a challenge. Our first workshop was for teachers in a special education setting and we were convinced that they would, at the very least, feel patronized. It didn't turn out that way; it seemed that the exercises we devised that used whole-body experiences really resonated with them.

Teachers commented that they had never experienced before how it might feel to their pupils. They admitted that because of deadlines and targets they often felt they had to 'move pupils along'. This was difficult because it would often cause a shutdown or a meltdown.

We continued to run workshops for teachers. The recurring message was that these kinesthetic whole-body exercises helped the participants to recognize and understand how their anxiety impacted on the children they worked with. The teachers experienced how their bodies and minds reacted to sensory overload. They realized that behaviour they saw as defiant, disobedient or challenging was in fact an expression of distress. It became evident to many participants that first there needed to be a change in themselves.

We recognized that we needed to find an approach for participants that would enable them to take one step back before trying to 'strategize' the autistic student because, in our experience, that does not work.

Tessa explained to me the approach she had learned when calming her son and it seemed that Honey, the spaniel, was to give us our biggest insight when creating Clear Time and the 3C Pathway.

Chapter 2

Creating the Practice

Clear Time and the 3C Pathway

'What is essential in engagement is the one-on-one interaction. The only thing you need is you.'

(Caldwell 2014, p.138)

The 3C Pathway is a simple relational approach that can revolutionize parenting. If parents struggle to connect with their autistic child, and subsequently the child struggles to trust and connect with them, the 3C Pathway and Clear Time is a wonderful way to explore the relationship and establish a bond that many parents may not have thought possible.

As parents and professionals, it was always our desire

to build reciprocal communication with the children we love and work with. It is the key to building a trusted relationship. We observed that, if we took two systematic steps back before we communicated, by simply connecting in a calm, open, authentic way, the child felt safe and seen. If we failed to do this, in our keenness to communicate, we saw communication failing and autistic children shutting down or 'melting' down, because of the pressure they felt to meet other people's needs.

The 3C Pathway was developed as a result of our work on the ground. We then followed the lead of the children, and when we became present, calmly 'tuning in' and emptying ourselves of our expectations, reciprocal communication happened. For many years, practitioners and parents have focused their work on changing the child's responses and behaviours, but we firmly believe that the change needed is with the practitioner or parent, not the child. This tuning in and emptying of ourselves we have called Clear Time, which has become a vital part of the 3C Pathway and fundamental to our work at Act for Autism.

Our main ethos is that parents and professionals need to empty themselves of expectations, be present, throw away their agenda, be caring, connected and calm and do what they have to do to be 'clear'.

The more we worked with professionals and parents, the more we saw that the 3C Pathway was having a dramatic effect. The main benefit is that it is a simple system that can be personalized.

We are not saying this is the only intervention, and you may recognize elements of intensive interaction and low-arousal techniques. The 3C Pathway combines what we see that works, and what we instinctively feel benefits the relationship an autistic child has with themselves and others. We have seen its positive effects time and again.

The link between the 3C Pathway and drama/acting is not obvious, but for those who are interested, we will explain it here. The 3Cs that we use as a therapeutic intervention are also core components of an actor's craft. An actor needs to understand all the nuances of communication to be able to confidently express words and emotions via their character and performance. To do this, they must authentically connect with their emotions and those of their fellow actors. They will also need to work on their physical state, so that they are calm and in control of their emotions. All actors can relate stories of stage fright associated with performance anxiety. To be able to assess their state and bring down their anxiety is, for an actor, a vital skill. For the actor and for us, as parents and teachers, communication without calm connection will feel inauthentic and will not create the reciprocal effect we crave.

Actors use breath control, body awareness and rhythmical physical exercises to work on their Communication, their Connection and to Calm themselves. We have adapted many of these exercises and we share them later in this book. We are not teaching autistic children to act or parents to be drama teachers. We have taken elements of our early practice as drama teachers and actors that we have seen to be very effective in our drama sessions for autistic students and simplified them into a therapeutic/healing practice that anyone can try.

Chapter 3

Connecting through Drama

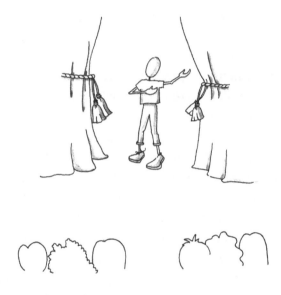

'When I play, I am free, we laugh and share; it's a nice feeling.'

(Louise, aged 12)

At Act for Autism, we use drama in everything we do. We run drama groups for young people, use drama techniques to engage our audiences in our training, and we adapt drama exercises to help participants walk in the shoes of an autistic person. The 3C Pathway includes many practices familiar to actors or drama practitioners. As an actor, you must be present, constantly changing your state and focusing on the best communication method to respond to, and affect, another person.

Maybe it's no coincidence that we both come from an acting background. Both of us trained in the dramatic arts, have taught drama, and acted professionally. It was not our conscious intention to unite the worlds of drama and autism, as that might suggest that we want children to act, but instinctively we brought what we have learned, and loved, about working in the field of the dramatic arts to our practice, and we see that it works.

If we were painters, we would have used art; if we were musicians, we would have used music; if we were dancers, we would have used dance; but we are drama professionals at heart, so using what we know and trust was the basis for our autism support. Tessa initially set up a drama group to help her son integrate socially with others in a safe place, and it was through the drama group that she saw the power of connection, calming and communication, the three Cs. More and more autistic children who had nowhere to go to interact safely without the risk of ridicule and rejection were attracted to the group. Tessa saw children's confidence grow and communication develop. It wasn't the aim of the group to intentionally focus on processing, interaction, communication, sensory processing and sensory integration – but these areas do develop during the children's time in the group.

Children felt safe to explore different aspects of social understanding and social skills (things that are instinctive for others) and they were allowed to stretch the muscle of being in relationship with their peers, who accepted them for who they were. All of these skills became something that they could take with them into other situations.

Jane gained similar insights while working in the school system where she was teaching drama. She saw young pupils thrive in her drama studio while struggling to engage and connect elsewhere in the school environment. In the drama studio, they could play, practise, fail and try again. Providing a fantastic learning environment, with a non-judgemental teacher, drama was often the only lesson where they felt safe and seen.

Drama sessions include warm-up games, breathing activities, role play, dressing-up and storytelling. These activities all have a part to play in the fun of the session, but they also subtly transform and become instructive. Warm-up games tell us what we need to know about the children's sensory issues that day and allow them to ground themselves in their bodies and in the setting. The breathing exercises help them learn how to self-regulate, power their voice, relax their bodies and clear their thinking. The turn-taking exercises help them to develop their attention and to work collaboratively and with compromise.

They are having fun and consequently they want to communicate with each other, and they want to interact, because they want the game to go well. Nobody asks them to meet someone else's expectations.

Autistic children also tell us they often find it hard to understand emotions – theirs and other people's – but through creating scenarios and characters in the role-play and storytelling exercises, they can explore emotions safely. For example, if we enact a social situation that they find difficult to interpret in everyday life, they can 'tap into' how it feels in the safety of an inclusive environment.

One of the examples of how we connect in drama club is 'News Time'. We always start with this. We sit in a circle and one of the children asks, 'Who's got news?' They then get to share something that has happened to them during the week. They are interacting, communicating and processing spontaneously. Because it is called 'News Time' rather than just asking what they have been up to, it feels less scary and more structured. No one is obliged to join in, but as the rhythm of the exercise and the playful nature is established, many children who arrive unable to contribute can end up wanting to take the lead.

When accessing drama as a connecting and comm-unication tool, you are safe because there is no 'wrong'. What you have is a platform for exploration. In some of the imaginative and dramatic role plays the children get to feel bigger, stronger, funnier, crazier in the safety of the game and in a trusted, playful environment. They explore and expand expression, so, as with any stretch, they grow. They grow in self-awareness, awareness of others, self-expression and self-regulation. These are things that many autistic people tell us they struggle with.

If you spend most of your life feeling anxious, trying to explore how you feel in a real-life situation can be almost impossible. You are trying to survive the communication, rather than thrive. In a drama group, you can explore reciprocity, the back and forth of shared communication, and practise the social communication skills that you find hard to access in life.

How we are feeling also comes into play when we learn. If we learn when calm, the learning is different from when we learn in a state of anxiety. The driver who has learned to drive, but every lesson was laced with anxiety, will probably remain an anxious driver. Their muscle memory was 'laid down' through elevated energy, or as it is often called, nervous energy. Our children are often learning new things through nervous energy. Drama helps our children to learn in a more relaxed state.

For autistic children, to be able to explore how they feel through drama means they are able, in part, to realign their muscle, sense and emotion memory. Research now tells us that neural pathways can, to some extent, be changed and rerouted.

We came to drama in our practice as an instinct; it was our way of connecting with the children we were working with. We see its effects in many immeasurable ways.

Chapter 4

Why Is Autism Hard to Understand?

'One thing is certain however: for many people, it's not autism that is a problem, but all the baggage that goes with it.'

(Fletcher-Watson and Happé 2019, p.39)

Some of the most common questions we still get asked by parents and professionals who love, live or work with autistic children, are:

- What is autism and why does my child behave differently from their peers?
- What is the best treatment?
- Will they get better?

As parents and practitioners, it can feel hopeless and frustrating not knowing why our children are struggling and what will work best. No one has yet come up with a conclusive, universally agreed reason for autism and the resulting behaviours. This is because autism is not one thing. Autism is different for everyone who experiences it. It's not a disease or a disorder that can be categorized by a set of specific markers. It's not visible so other people may not make immediate adjustments when needed. It is a condition that has existed forever, and researchers and others are still seeking answers to many questions. What is known is that if other people recognize and understand the individual and the demands made, and the setting and context are adjusted accordingly, then many autistic children and young people flourish and are successful.

What we do know now is that autism is a neurological condition that presents itself uniquely in each person. People are autistic because of their unique brain wiring system, and because of this difference in wiring, they are likely to see, hear, feel and experience the world differently from their peers. There are common challenges, but each person's experience is different, and this is one of the reasons why understanding autism is so hard for parents and professionals. It is also difficult because we don't sense the world as they do, and because for an autistic person, sharing personal insights into how their world seems is a real challenge.

But if you think that understanding autism is tough for you, let's not forget that being autistic and not being understood by others is a greater struggle. The difficulties with autism stem not just because of the specifics of the condition but because autism exists within the context of a universal lack of understanding.

When we talk about the condition of autism, we are not just talking about a medical set of facts relating to how a condition may present. Autism as a condition is much more than a label attributed to a set of behaviours. Autism and how it presents sits in the context of the individual's environment, personality and lived experience. This is then exacerbated because of confusions, myths and misunderstandings that have existed for years.

Misunderstandings originate from historical inaccuracies that, since autism was first documented, have often been published as truths. Additionally, it comes from a medical profession that, over time, has debated and changed the diagnostic criteria. When professionals do not agree on the root cause or the symptoms of autism, this is problematic.

The historical narrative and the pathologizing of autistic traits have meant that professionals have tended to focus on deficits and weaknesses. If we use an asset-based thinking model, which encourages thinking about the potential of the autistic brain, we begin to see more positive outcomes.

For many years, these factors combined have resulted in a narrative that has not helped to provide clarity for autistic individuals or the wider society. We must consider the autistic condition and how to appropriately support people in the context of this misunderstanding. We should also consider how that has impacted on autistic individuals' lived experience. Autism, and its diverse neurology, is one thing, but how autistic individuals have been viewed, how they are treated and how they navigate through a society not geared to them is another.

For example, an autistic child who is born into a family that is wholly accepting of difference and diversity and is calm and patient and who has access to support that is person-centred, plus a social network and education system that is equally patient, calm and accepting, will have a different experience from that of an autistic child who is born into a family where difference and diversity are not accepted. One child is living with acceptance and the other in a social system that stigmatizes people who are different.

Imagine the autism diagnosis is similar in both children, but the presentation of the autism will be relative to the lived experience. This causes the stigmatized child's autism to be more challenging to live with. It will not necessarily mean the condition itself is worse.

It is only in recent years that academics, researchers and practitioners have come to the realization that autistic people should be leading the conversation on what might be helpful. We have done 'to' and 'for' rather than 'with' them, and failed to consult them, for too long.

We believe that to really understand autism and empathetically connect with it, it is vital to recognize that autism sits within these various contexts – the historical context, the medical context, the social context and the family context.

While this is not a history book, it might be helpful to be aware of how the autism narrative developed over the last century or so. What is useful to notice is that there is no single, agreed view on what causes autism or how best to treat and support autistic people. Over the years, medics and scientists have published disturbing and contradictory theories, often taken as fact or truth.

1911 Swiss psychiatrist Eugen Bleuler is the first to use the term 'schizophrenia' and connect autistic behaviours with this condition.

1920s 'Symptoms' of autism relate to diet, so 'patients' are given biochemical treatments and diet supplements.

1924 Child psychiatrist Grunya Sukhareva notices a clear distinction between schizophrenic traits and the traits of her young patients; she sees their challenges as neurological rather than behavioural and wants to create positive environments in which they can thrive. (If the significance of her work had been fully taken on board at the time, rather than overlooked, autistic people could have avoided a great deal of suffering.)

1930s Electroconvulsive therapy is used to correct 'antisocial' behaviour in autistic people and others.

1940s 'Autism' is first used as a term to describe children who have severe emotional and social issues. Leo Kanner, a child psychiatrist, establishes the first accepted definition of autism: 'a lack of affective contact, fascination with objects, desire for sameness and non-communication language before 30 months of age'. Around this time, German scientist, Hans Asperger works with a cohort of young children with similar behaviours, but the children are verbal, and he observes that these children can be highly productive and content if calm and self-directed.

1950s Austrian psychologist Bruno Bettelheim writes *The Empty Fortress: Infantile Autism and the Birth of the Self*, which promotes the idea that autism is caused by cold and uncaring mothers, coining the phrase 'refrigerator mother'. He suggests the immediate removal of the child from the parents.

1960s Testing of treatments including pain and punishment to correct 'antisocial' behaviour are introduced, including LSD to inhibit serotonin, with the idea that altering the autistic patient's perception will alleviate symptoms.

1965 The first advocacy groups are set up to support autistic people, but their reach is limited.

1970s Psychiatrist Lorna Wing talks about autism as a spectrum and introduces the *Triad of Impairments*.

1980s Behavioural therapy becomes a more common treatment for autistic children. Autism is finally categorized separately from schizophrenia.

1990 'Holding therapy' is introduced, based on the idea that the child and mother don't have a secure attachment: a child is restrained, forced to perform various tasks and rewarded if they do so.

1996 Temple Grandin writes *Emergence*, her account of her life. She is one of the first self-advocates.

1998 *The Lancet* publishes an article stating that the measles, mumps and rubella (MMR) vaccine is a suggested cause of autism.

2003 Bernard Rimland and Stephen Edelson write *Recovering Autistic Children*, suggesting autism can be 'cured'.

2013 The diagnostic manual, *DSM-5*, classifies all autism subcategories (e.g. Asperger's syndrome) under the one label of autism spectrum disorder.

This is by no means the full history. The rewrites and updates are constant and often contradictory. Even today we have a vast array of conflicting beliefs about causes, interventions and prognosis.

The first media representation, of any note, was the 1988 film *Rain Man*. In this film, starring Dustin Hoffman and Tom Cruise, autism was represented in the character of Raymond as a disorder that rendered someone non-verbal, anxious, fixated, detached, isolated and dysfunctional. It was a beautifully told story and the character that we felt most compassion for was Raymond. However, it set a narrative about autism that did not wholly represent autistic individuals.

When a large-budget Hollywood movie says, 'This is what autism is' and there is little or no other representation, it goes without saying that that's what people will think autism is. Until the autistic community was taken seriously as the advocates for their own condition and given a voice, we only had what was reported in medical journals, news articles and films. This for many years has been heavily weighted towards autism being a problem for society that had to be hidden away or eradicated.

Imagine you had a condition, of any kind, and the world you lived in did not understand it. Clinicians tried to 'cure' you, parents were told there was no hope and you should be taken to an institution, and the world never considered that you may have something to contribute.

Whatever your condition, how would you feel? The condition and its challenges may not be at the centre of your issues; rather the psychological effects of other people's views and their subsequent treatment of you become the issue. The autistic community is not the only group of people to be mistreated, misrepresented and marginalized, but the difference is that in other communities there have been fierce advocates who over time have galvanized support, challenged perceptions and held society to account, insisting on greater representation.

Why did advocates not rise up in the autistic community earlier on in its history?

One may suggest it is because some of the core challenges in autism are spoken communication, self-awareness and dealing with pressure. These are all skills required for competent advocacy. Also, maybe it's because no one actually asked them.

> Through all the changes and new paradigms, one factor remained constant: the perspective of autistic people was consistently erased from the narrative. (Fletcher-Watson and Happé 2019, p.25)

Thankfully, we are moving on and there are now so many brilliant accounts written by young autistic people and adults about their lived experience. It is from these and scientific advances that we are learning so much more about the diversity of the autism spectrum, and the range of experiences that have contributed to an individual's successes or challenges.

However, the residue of the systematic misrepresentation still makes living with and understanding autism harder than it needs to be. In all our work, it is our intention to simplify the confusion, not only for the autistic individuals, but for those who support them. Once we understand and accept this chequered history, we can then move on and start to understand the autistic condition itself.

It is our desire, with this book, to help your understanding of autism so you can be the greatest support possible. To do that, we have enlisted, where we can, the autistic community and drawn on the work we have had the privilege to do alongside them and through the relationships we have forged with them. This book does not promise to give you an answer to all the questions you have. It aims to give you simple, effective ways to connect calmly and communicate with the autistic people in your life, so that they can reveal to you what their world feels like and what they need most from you.

Chapter 5

Understanding Autism as a Sensory Difference and the Link to Anxiety

'There are times when situations feel downright hopeless for us – our daily lives are so full of tough stuff to tackle.'

(Higashida 2007, p.53)

The wasp story

We start with two versions of the same scenario.

Scenario A: Josh, aged seven, is eating ice cream in a café with his mum, Lucy. A wasp is buzzing round their table. He jumps up and knocks his bowl to the floor to get away from it, waving his arms about as it buzzes in his face; despite Lucy's efforts to calm him, he gets stung and starts screaming. Lucy tries to comfort Josh, but he's really distressed and can't calm down. He knocks his chair over. People start to look over, disgruntled that their peaceful afternoon is being disturbed, but once they realize what's happened, they look on in sympathy – everyone knows how horrible it is to get stung. The manager comes over and asks if she can help. She apologizes for the wasp and says they'll look into getting some wasp traps in future. A woman on an adjacent table pulls antihistamine cream from her bag, and the manager comes over with a new ice cream for Josh. Lucy realizes that people looking on from other tables aren't annoyed, but empathetic. An elderly man leaving the café comes over and congratulates Lucy for dealing with Josh so calmly.

Scenario B: Same café, different day. Amelia is with her dad, Simon. He's ordered a sandwich for Amelia, but it's slathered in mayonnaise and the bread has gone a little soggy. Amelia pushes her plate away, but it knocks her juice over, and the cup falls onto the floor. She starts moaning, pulling away from Simon as he tries to calm her. Amelia stands up and pushes the table. Her chair falls back and knocks the neighbouring table. The people at that table get up and move, complaining under their breath. An elderly woman tuts loudly. Simon tries to get Amelia to sit down and try a bit of the sandwich, but her screaming grows louder and she throws the sandwich onto the floor. An elderly woman on another table starts talking loudly about spoiled children who don't eat what's put in front of them. Amelia sinks down, starts crying and banging her fists on the floor. A man with a laptop near the door asks the manager if she can do something about the noise. Before the manager can investigate, Simon has picked Amelia up – not easy, as she's seven – and taken her out, still crying. As he leaves, he hears a couple commenting to their grandchild about how he is a good boy and doesn't behave like that.

In Scenario A, the customers and manager empathize with the distress of a wasp sting and see that Josh's response is understandable. It's a 'normal' response to a strong, unexpected sensory stimulus. The initial response is irritation, but this soon gives way to empathy.

The level of noise and disruption is exactly the same in Scenario B, but there is no wasp. For Amelia, who is autistic, everyday sensations can feel as distressing as a wasp sting. Were the lights too bright, the sandwich too soggy, the music too loud and the smells from the kitchen overwhelming? When an autistic child feels the pain of a new, irregular and sudden input, whether it's sound, light or taste, they are often met with judgement rather than empathy and consideration. This lack of empathetic response when it's most needed can make autistic people feel that their world is full of threats, and full of hostile people looking on and judging. This judgement of others, rather than understanding, can increase parents' stress too, which can then affect their ability to deal appropriately with their child in distress.

But maybe you want to know why the sensory system is different and why this leads to what is too often called 'challenging behaviours' which are, we feel, mistakenly identified as someone's autism rather than being seen as a response to sensory overload and the environment. These reactions to sensory stimulus need to be understood in the context of differences in the wiring of the autistic brain.

> Neuroimaging can't tell us everything. But it can tell us a lot. A technology that can look at a part of the brain and address, what does it look like and what does it do? It can also answer a couple of bonus questions: How does the autistic brain look different from the normal brain? And what does an autistic brain do differently than a normal brain? (Grandin 2013, p.23)

Whatever we commit to the page today may well be superseded by new research tomorrow, such is the pace of research in the field of autism. However, we wanted to share some current thinking about the interconnectivity of the brain and the senses, and how there are differences in these connections within the autistic brain.

Neuroscientists have fast-evolving technological wizardry at their fingertips, meaning that experts in the field continue to 'drill down' and discover new things daily. They are constantly searching for ideas on how the brain works.

As we have said before, while we and the scientists are looking for the answers there is a child or young person needing our emotional understanding, so regardless of the ever-moving science, we need to be 'sleuthing' for what makes our individual tick. This is with a view to empathetically connecting with our children and therefore gaining as much information as we can about why our children can struggle. We believe this gives us as parents a greater ability to advocate for our children.

We love this quote from Ralph-Axel Muller in *The New York Times*. Neither of us claims to be a neuroscientist, so this really helped us better understand the differences in connectivity in the autistic brain and the sensory system:

> Impairments that we see in autism seem to be partly due to different parts of the brain talking too much to each other. You need to lose connections in order to develop a fine-tuned system of brain networks, because if all parts of the brain talk to all parts of the brain all you get is noise. (*The New York Times* 2014)

When we are born, our brains have more than 86 billion brain cells (or neurons) which pass signals to each other via as many as 1000 trillion connection points (or synapses). A synapse is a gap at the end of each neuron, which uses chemical messengers (or neurotransmitters) to pass information to the next neuron. From the age of about 18 months, the brain starts to prune these neurons and synapses. Eventually about fifty per cent of the neurons and synapses are reduced or replaced by more complex and efficient structures. Experts think that one of the contributing factors in autism is that this pruning and changing happens differently in the autistic brain, leaving too many or too few synapses, and differences in the way that the neurons and synapses are laid down. In addition, there can be chemical imbalances which can cause problems in the transmission of information. Researchers are also exploring how the different regions in the autistic brain talk to each other, with regions close to each other talking to each other too much, and regions that are further apart not talking to each other enough.

A child can experience hypersensitivity when there hasn't been enough pruning and they are getting too much sensory information or 'noise', or hyposensitivity when there has been too much pruning and the different parts of the brain don't talk to each other enough. Both states can be problematic, as this can lead to the misinterpretation of everyday sensory information. It is very hard to organize or act on information productively when it is transmitted in this way and there are gaps in the information, or too much information. This can lead to what we call 'cognitive chaos'.

Now, those of us who have travelled on the London Underground would probably agree it is a noisy, busy place. Let's just visualize the brain as the London Underground.

The London Underground relies on seamless connections between the stations, the trains, the train driver and the signals. Stations are connected by train tracks, and train drivers drive the train along the track to the next station – the drivers are controlled by the signals.

What would happen if there were too many signals or too few? Or if the drivers were getting mixed signals, they wouldn't know what to do, and eventually there might be a crash. They would be confused and unable to process the information quickly enough to make a decision. Ultimately, the drivers would probably get to their destination, but it is going to take longer, and they may get there via a different route.

The neurotransmitters that are transmitting to and from the brain also acquire and pass on information from our sensory system. Our sensory receptors are present throughout our whole body from our fingertips to our organs. The system that helps with the organizing of the senses – the central nervous system – does a fantastic job of helping to conduct all the information to the stations in the brain.

We can imagine that decisions are like a conversation between our head and our heart. Senses are a little like energy fields that help the body and the brain to work out what we need. It takes a nanosecond for a sensory experience to reach the brain, via the heart. The brain then sends a signal back to the body, via the heart, and that's when we interpret and act on the information.

In other words, the senses help us to understand our physical experiences. For example, if you put your hand on something hot, the sensation is transmitted to the brain where it is interpreted. From this we can then build our memories and create our perceptions. This information is also stored in our muscle memory and we then recall that memory when it is needed to help us navigate our world.

Think about learning a new skill. Eventually our body takes over and we don't have to think about how we do it. For example, the driver of that train will have learned how to drive the train and now drives it on automatic pilot. Try to imagine how hard it must be to function when we can't trust the sensory signals our body is sending us. Our head is signalling one way and our heart another way. If we try to empathize and 'walk in the autistic child's shoes', we can start to understand why our children can be so destabilized by the mixed signals that their sensory system and their brain are communicating to them.

If we now spend a moment visualizing and imagining navigating the world when the signals we are getting are like a chaotic malfunctioning London Underground system, we may be able to empathize more with our children's inability to access the world as efficiently as other children.

Now imagine your brain feels as if it is also rush hour, and suddenly the signal boards are flashing misinformation or hieroglyphics, sirens sound and then the lights go out.

You would probably just want everything to stop. That's when we witness shutdown or meltdown in our children, but it doesn't happen out of defiance or temper. It happens out of anxiety, fear and sensory overload. Therefore, it is a little unreasonable to label what happens in a meltdown or shutdown as 'challenging behaviour'. It is much fairer to call this reaction a 'distress signal'. Most of us would become distressed if we had to spend our time in these circumstances.

We can only imagine how it feels to be overwhelmed by our own system. It is also important to remember that there are variations of differences, and every autistic person experiences the world differently, as no one connectivity pattern applies to every autistic person.

Let's now take one step further in trying to understand the importance of the information we get from our senses. If we revisit the experience of putting our hand on something hot, those receptors we talked about, which are located all over our bodies, go straight to work to help us build procedural memories so that we don't do it again.

A signal goes to the brain via the heart. The heart says, 'Hey brain, how am I going to react? Do I run away, kick the oven or pretend it's not happening?'

The brain says, 'Heart, slow down. Running away won't help, the pain is happening, and don't kick the oven – it won't help.'

So, we just slow ourselves down and take in what has happened, how much it hurt, and we ask, 'If I encounter another hotplate, what will I feel?'

Heart and brain agree and say, 'I think I will feel frightened of hotplates in the future, so that's a job well learned. Unless I want to feel fright and pain, I'm not putting my hand on any more hotplates!'

Again, this is a crude analogy, but it does illustrate how a non-autistic brain and body interpret, gather and store experiences and perceptions through the information that the senses contribute. It is difficult to make sense of what is happening to you if you are experiencing cognitive chaos.

How possible is it to deal with the experience of putting our hand on a hotplate when we are experiencing cognitive chaos?

When we are told that autistic individuals find it hard to understand emotions, both theirs and other people's, we must explore how complicated it is for the autistic brain and body to give consistent and useful information. If you don't get consistent information, it is very hard to trust yourself or 'read' other people. This can make you very anxious and consequently also unable to read yours and other people's emotions.

There are many theories on why a high proportion of autistic individuals suffer from anxiety. It is important to understand that anxiety is perhaps partly due to these differences in brain wiring and sensory perception. There are, nevertheless, many different factors, including the environment, which can also contribute to someone struggling with anxiety.

Anxiety generates both mental and physical symptoms. Anxiety starts with 'unhelpful thoughts', we catastrophize, and our minds search for what is making us fearful. Anxiety can also be caused by stress or can trigger stress. If you have not built up a repertoire of emotion and sensory experiences that you can call on to calm your fears, it can be almost impossible to stop anxiety building in the mind and body. You will then exhibit stress symptoms and thus the cycle continues.

This can be exhausting as 'all you are getting is noise' and then, to top it all, a well-meaning person tries to fix the situation.

The situation is not ultimately the problem. Understanding how the autistic person is experiencing and negotiating their own physiological and cognitive state is what is important; we need to try to help them to navigate their world. This help can be as simple as not being yet another noise.

We have established that the brain and the senses help us to navigate the world. Again, we want to dig a little deeper to find out about how the autonomic nervous system – the part of our system that acts unconsciously and regulates heart rate and other bodily functions – can also be added to the list of differences that can exacerbate anxiety and cognitive chaos in an autistic individual.

Autism, as understood at this moment in time, is the outcome of a constellation of different complex bodily mechanisms. Neuroception – the way our brain automatically helps us to keep out of trouble, without involving the thinking parts of our brain – can be constantly 'switched on' in the autistic brain and body. This part of our system, the bit that senses things at a primal level, is also the part that keeps us safe, that listens out for danger, without us being consciously aware of it.

Let's imagine you are walking down a dark alley on your own, with no torch or phone, and you hear a twig snap behind you. You look behind you, you see a shadow, it disappears. At this point, you realize that your heart is beating faster, and you then realize that you have created a story in your head that you are in danger from someone who is following you.

If asked later about your experience, you would relive the experience and probably name how it made you feel (emotion). Simply put, this is one of the ways we create emotions, from our senses. This experience would then be a part of your sense/emotion memory. It was your neuroception/instinct that started the story – the part of you that you can't control. This part of your system just loves seeking out danger. This is great as we need to survive and thrive, but unfortunately our autistic children spend most of their time just surviving because they are not building sense memories that can help them to navigate the world. Within this system, of which we have no control, our adrenalin is turned on and this tells us to stay and fight, run away or immobilize ourselves. It is this immobilization pathway that is our last resort when all other forms of connection or communication fail. This is when shutdown, collapse and dissociation happen, just like the animal that plays dead so that the predator walks on by. Autistic children often operate from this pathway rather than the pathway that works out what to do. This can have positive and negative outcomes. Autistic children can often have highly tuned instincts. That's why, for example, they can sense our anxiety so acutely, which causes them to disconnect. So, what happens when these systems that travel up and down and round and round the body are working well? There is flow, smooth running operations, the heart asks the brain what to do, the brain gives a good answer and on we go.

However, what happens when there is a problem and you are continually operating from your fight, flight or immobilize instinct? Consider the scenario from earlier; you are going to be attacked by the man in the dark alley. At this point, all that good energy that is keeping you contented turns into instinctive high-alert energy. When the high-alert energy is higher in the mix than the thinking part of the brain, your autonomic response kicks in. This would explain, in part, why anxiety is the most common co-occurring condition in autism.

Another cause of anxiety is faster blood flow. Researchers have been able to magnify, as little tiny impulses, the motion of the heart sending blood to the brain. This movement is smaller than the width of a piece of hair. These researchers have identified the movement in an autistic brain as being infinitesimally faster. This faster moving blood travels through, among other areas of the brain, the amygdala (which is partially responsible for emotions), which may, in part, explain why many autistic individuals can experience heightened emotions that they find hard to control. Researchers have also stated that the heart beats faster in most autistic individuals and this makes it hard to instinctively self-regulate. If practised, self-regulation in the form of heartbeat exercises can bring down the heart rate by 'putting a brake' on the heart.

It is through our work with children, teachers, healthcare professionals, parents and carers that we first started to notice how bringing down the heart rate can be extremely helpful both for the parent and the child. We always suggest calming yourself by tuning into your heart rate before you connect. Consequently, we have explored and created heartbeat exercises that help to decrease the resting heart rate – see Chapter 12.

Now we must start to 'walk in the shoes' of these children and try to empathize with the exhaustion and anxiety that leads to and comes from meltdown or shutdown. 'Walking in the shoes' of someone means working as hard as you can to understand the perspective and lived experience of the person you are supporting, imagining what it must feel like to be them and how they experience the world. If you can do this, you begin to have what we call an empathetic connection.

We have gained a lot of our intellectual understanding from research and science, but we gained our empathetic under-standing from listening to and accepting the experiences of autistic individuals, once they trusted us and felt able to share their perceptions.

Chapter 6

What Autistic Individuals Say about Their Sensory Experience – Personal Accounts

'Processing all the information needed to make sense of the world can be overwhelming.'

(Pernille, aged 18)

Two of the things we really wanted to include in this book were case studies and personal testimony. For us the voice of the children and young people we work with and care for cannot be underestimated when trying to empathize with someone who is autistic.

Paul, who is 27 years old, talks about his experience of his sensory system. What is also important to note in Paul's testimony is his brilliant ability to intellectually understand his sensory challenges.

Autism and sensory issues can present themselves in many different and varied ways; not all presentations of sensory issues are the same and that is a major factor in understanding or lack thereof. Stereotypes around autism persist so one may just think of 'sensory hypersensitivities' and leave it at that. However, in the broader realities we must look at perception, which is the awareness of sense, regardless whether the sensory organs are intact or not. This is called agnosia (loss of perceptual knowledge), in which a person may be face blind (prosopagnosia), object blind (simultagnosia) or meaning blind (semantic agnosia). These can have an impact on bonding, friendships and mentalizing, and the person who has this profile may have more kinesthetic ways of navigating the world.

You can have others who may be in pain or body blind (body agnosia) and may struggle to map their body in space in their environment, may self-harm, struggle to regulate emotions, understand internal pressures when toileting, and not have a 'switch-off point'. All these things aren't to do with low intelligence or 'mental retardation' but the nervous system and awareness of the senses. Let's start looking at autism in a more three-dimensional manner.

Paul goes on to describe, in vivid detail, what his world can feel like from a sensory perspective on any given day.

> How can you tell, how can I know? Everybody has them [senses] but mine are like going around a round-about that gets clogged up – frankly awful, too much electricity, it overloads. I go into automatic mode – pretend everything is fine: sight, sound, touch, smell, taste, how I balance, what I feel. It's hard. If I am out and it's sunny, I can't tell which is a hole in the pavement and which is a shadow. Every noise is noticed; I go into a café, everything is heard, and it's all got to be processed, worked out. What's information I need and don't need? The smell of the café – it had been painted a week ago but when I walk in it feels like I am in a sauna, the smell makes me hot. My socks feel as if I am walking on nails, there are labels in my trousers, the seams hurt. I can't process all the feelings as well as all the other stuff that I've noticed. I don't know what I feel.
>
> Going out is supposed to be a reward – no, I want to hide in the corner, so there's not so much to process. Face blindness, so I can't recognize you when I see you again, then next time you see me you think I'm rude. I am anxious all day because of having too much to deal with and process and also because people react badly when I do speak as I think I appear odd. So then I can become non-verbal. All I'm trying to do is work out what bits of the sensory information I'm getting are helpful. It's only now I'm older that I can do that. For most of my childhood everyone just assumed I didn't like people and liked being on my own. That's not the

case, but partly because that happened, I always find social situations really hard.

If we want to understand what Paul is articulating, we must accept that there are differences in brain wiring, the nervous system and therefore sensory processing. We must listen and learn from the experts, the autistic experts. Even if the autistic person in your life is not as articulate as Paul, they will be communicating their truth in their own unique way, and if we can connect calmly, they will trust us and in their communication we can learn more than we could ever learn from the 'expert' experts.

Rosa, who is 22 years old, talks about how she regulates herself:

I find it is important to keep my nervous system as relaxed as possible as my senses are over-sensitive. Other people speaking loudly over each other, loud music on top of other people talking and background noise, buzzing, car noise and electronic sounds can feel very enclosing for me. I feel like I need to get away from these noises and can sometimes get very tense and quiet when there are these extra noises. In terms of regulating my emotions around these extra sensory sensitivities, it can be challenging as my emotions feel very strong within my body, I can get a hot feeling over my body which I then want to also escape from, plus my head begins to feel overloaded and then numb, which is a challenge. I have found that getting away from the extra noise, taking a breath or putting a pause in the situation and removing or excusing myself from it for a moment does help to prevent me going into an unnecessarily high stressful state and meltdown.

Rosa describes how acutely the emotions she is feeling manifest as a physical sensation. Again, we must understand how debilitating this can be. This is her reality, and regularly experiencing these sensations can impact on her navigation of the world. Contrary to the common perception of a lack of self-awareness or emotional intelligence in autistic people, Rosa displays a sophisticated understanding of her challenges and has created resourceful, self-regulatory strategies.

Jordan, an autistic advocate and special educational needs and disability learning support assistant, describes how his sensory integration can impact on him. He manages to hold down a full-time job but as you read his testimony, imagine how exhausting this can be.

> Negative sensory experiences can be really damaging for an individual. A particularly bad sensory experience I had was when training to work in education.
>
> I was walking down a staircase and a fire alarm suddenly started ringing out. It was a loud siren that was very high-pitched with different tones. I have always found fire alarms tricky. As I was on a staircase, there was not just one alarm point, but six! Six alarms screeching out in an echoey staircase. The sudden shock of them sent me into a sheer panic, making me scream to be louder than them. Knowing I can be louder helps me block the sound out and feel safe. I was not able to be louder than six alarms, as well as the sound of all the bells ringing in the corridors. Having to deal not only with all that sound and process it, but also with bright, flashing white and red lights on each alarm was a challenge. The flashes of light

mixed in with the loud sounds and my inability to regulate made it feel like my eyes were burning. My thought process was to leave the building not because there could be a fire, but because I was frightened and needed to escape this sensory overload. As I ran down the never-ending stairs, I was trying to cover my eyes from all the flashing lights, while covering my ears from the noise, while carrying two heavy bags, while holding on to the hand rail for support as I felt very ungrounded without balance.

I realized nobody else was leaving their lessons to evacuate, making me confused as well as more distressed. I felt so alone in a situation when I really needed help. When I got to the bottom of the stairs there were two different exits. Exit one was to walk down a dark corridor, past a ringing bell and out of the fire exit. Exit two was to open another door and go through the main reception area, where I know someone there could help me. I chose exit two, where I knew I could get help. As I opened the door, I noticed something moving. It was an emergency fire shutter coming down. There was no way I was going down the corridor with the bell, so I threw my bags under this shutter and jumped under. The fire shutter continued to drop and I landed on my knee. As I was in a state of overload, I hardly felt it until I had got the help I needed and left the building. I was then in a lot of pain and had bruised my knee rather badly, but I did not know anything about it at the time because I was having that sensory overload.

Sensory overloads like this are terrifying. You feel out of control, trapped, in danger; there is a sense of impending doom, with no end in sight. Sensory overloads are not pleasant, but with the right support they can be managed.

Luca describes how he feels his anxiety through his senses:

To help me cope with the fear of not understanding new rules, I always ask someone (be it a teacher or friend) who I feel comfortable talking to and this makes me feel at ease. In general, anxiety expresses itself in different forms. Sometimes, thoughts manifest in my head which can make it difficult to focus on one thing at one time; at other (most) times, I get 'butterflies' in my stomach which raises my adrenaline levels, and in the long run this makes me feel exhausted as the tension rises and falls suddenly without warning.

These testimonies are just four different perspectives, but even within this sample we can see how important it is to treat each person as an individual.

Chapter 7

The Eight Senses and How They Impact on a Child's Experience

'When I'm overloaded, I shut myself in the cupboard with my duvet and make myself enclosed. I pretend that's the only world there is; it's a very small world and helps me calm down.'

(George, aged 14)

There is much debate as to how many senses we have. Numbers vary from the five main senses – **sight**, **hearing**, **taste**, **smell** and **touch** – to eight when you add **proprioception**, **vestibular system** and **interoception**.

However, scientists are now reporting that there are far more – between 14 and 21 senses. A commonly held definition of a sense is a group of sensory receptors that react to a physical phenomenon.

Some researchers have divided the senses, which might explain the differences of opinion on how many senses there are. Sight, for example, is divided into sub-senses, where different kinds of receptors are present, one for colour and one for brightness/tone. Following that theory, sight becomes two senses. This theory would explain why Paul finds it hard to define a shadow from a hole but has no problem defining colours.

Exploring this theory further, we taste with different receptors, one each for sweet, salty, sour, bitter, and umami, which detects tastes found in meats and some artificial flavourings.

Touch is not just touch. It is also governed by receptors that give the signals for different touches, pressure, temperature, pain and itchiness! Understanding our temperature regulation is a very important part of our survival. In autism, the receptors for hot and cold and the thermoreceptors in the brain that are responsible for monitoring internal body temperature often seem to be differently wired.

There are so many ways in which we hear, requiring different receptors. Detecting vibrations along a medium, such as air or water, that is in contact with your eardrum, is a very different experience to hearing music, for example. Rosa experiencing sound and anxiety as a heat within her body can be better understood if we acknowledge the possible differences in her thermoreceptors and auditory receptors.

Smell is a sensor related to a chemical reaction and combines with taste to produce flavours. The sensory system is a complex system that, like so many parts of our anatomy, is still not fully understood. This is especially the case in autism.

Now let's explore the lesser known of the big eight – proprioception. This sense is used all the time without us having any idea that it is happening. Our proprioception tells us where our body is in space, and where our body parts are in relation to each other.

If you close your eyes and touch your nose, you are testing your proprioception. The objective of the exercise is to touch your nose on the first try. Take another example: you are feeling in your pocket for something. You can distinguish, by touch, a sticky sweet from a paper clip without looking at it; that's your proprioception doing its job. There is also the receptor for keeping your equilibrium. It keeps you balanced and able to sense body movements, acceleration and change of direction.

We are not yet at the end of the big eight and you can see how many chances there are in one human being for there to be slight or significant differences from the basic human template. When your vestibular system is malfunctioning, you literally may not be able to tell up from down. Or, if you have ever been in a maze or a labyrinth, you probably found that you lost your sense of direction. If your system is a little wobbly, you will probably find it hard to judge where a chair is as you try to sit down on it.

The sense that appears to play a significant part in the autistic challenge is interoception. This, simply described, is the internal sensory system that helps us to feel, and then interpret and understand, what is happening inside us. The receptors are in our organs and they help us to know when we are hungry, thirsty, hot or cold, and give us the signals that tell us how fast our heart is beating. After we have felt the sensation, the receptors kick in and tell the brain what we are feeling. We then gain the cognitive understanding of our internal state.

It is then that we make our decisions about how to help ourselves; for example, if we are hot, we take off our coat. We use this to self-regulate and we do it all the time without even thinking about it. Think back to the autonomic nervous system, that part of us that we have no control over. Also, think back to how the autistic individual experiences their sensory world differently.

Some of the differences in sensory processing can manifest in sensations and signals becoming mixed up (again, it is possible that Rosa's interoceptive system gives her mixed signals). An itch may feel painful and pain feels like an itch. If we imagine how that might impact on someone on a daily basis, we can start to 'walk in their shoes'. This makes it easier to accept their truth and connect with their sensory world. In this way, we can start to sleuth for clues about the emotional impact of sensory processing differences.

Cast your mind back to the dark alley sense/emotion exercise earlier in Chapter 5. Your body signalled to you that you were in danger. Your breathing sped up and you became aware of your elevated heart rate. What if you do not feel any fear because you don't recognize that you are tense, your breathing is shallow, and your heart rate elevated? You could be fearless. This could make you vulnerable and mean that your response to the situation is inappropriate.

If you are feeling thirsty, you take a drink. If you feel

hungry, you eat a snack. If you need the loo, you find one. What if your body interprets that empty stomach and full bladder as a need to move faster, to run and jump up and down?

Through these brief examples, you can start to understand why we feel interoceptive differences are so important to tune into. If your child reacts differently, trust that communication, unpick it, but not before you have calmly connected with your child through breathing and heartbeat work.

Remember, if you immediately try to solve or 'fix it', you are just going to be more noise. If we as parents and carers don't tread softly, we will not obtain the information we need in order to support our child's self-discovery and ultimate self-knowledge.

Through performing observational studies, researchers (Addabbo *et al.* 2018) speculate that a baby as young as 12–27 days will attempt to copy the caregiver's smile or facial gestures. They also suggest that interactional synchrony, reciprocal give-and-take, plays a vital part in the development of empathy, self-regulation and symbol use (in the form of words, sounds, gestures or visual images). Studies have also revealed that repeated reciprocal gestures can help build organizational skills.

If we consider all that we now know about differences in brain wiring and sensory processing, imagine, how hard it must be for the autistic baby to reciprocally respond. Many parents have told us that one of the things they remember about the early months of their children's lives is the lack of engagement, the lack of connection they felt with their baby. There was little initiation, and when they did lead, there were varying degrees of engagement. If we imagine the complicated sensory input that the baby must process, and then we add our movement and voice into the mix, it is easy to understand why the autistic baby has greater challenges to face in order to communicate effectively.

The trouble is, we find ourselves in need of responses and prompts. It is hardwired into our DNA and when natural responses don't occur, we can find it hard and our input and responses can subtly change psychologically and physically. We may, for example, become more persistent or withdraw emotionally. Because of the way their sensory system operates, our children can sense this on a level that is difficult to appreciate.

It is hard to feel that you may have missed some windows of opportunity in your child's development and that you may have connected differently had you understood the sensory processing differences inherent in your child.

However, to date, there is no empirical evidence or scientific research that unequivocally states how best to relate to an autistic baby. Whatever we did or do as parents, it is instinctive, and we should not attribute blame to ourselves. We are all human and although we may feel that we didn't do enough, we can now look at the situation from a different perspective, the perspective of first changing our communication mode before we try to strategize. We subscribe to the adage 'You only know what you know when you know it.'

We have witnessed, more than once, cases of allegedly non-verbal children and young people articulating extra-ordinarily complex thought processes once they feel safe and in rhythm and in tune with their reciprocal partner and once they are better able to regulate their sensory system. We were also challenged by an autistic parent who divulged to us, and the parent group she was attending, that she had been non-verbal until the age of six.

She couldn't completely explain why, but one of the things that struck us was her disclosure that she 'didn't have any time to articulate her thoughts as she was too busy with what she now understood to be sensory overload'. She was now a forensic police investigator, who had solved 24 out of 28 unsolved murder investigations that her superiors had assigned her. One could only marvel as she regaled us with the details of how she had done this. She had the ability to read the hard copy of a case from 1978 and not only remember all the details, but then synthesize everything she had retained and come up with an answer. She had found her own strategies for coping with sensory overload and once she had done this there was no stopping her.

We include this case, not because our children are destined to be high-flying police personnel, renowned inventors or musical geniuses, but because it would be foolish of us to assume that non-conventional communication means no cognitive, social or emotional progress.

Sometimes, our children need to navigate their sensory world before they can cope with communication. Progress will be happening, it is just different – a different speed and a different mode – and it won't hit the prescribed child developmental milestones. Ultimately, hard as it is, we must empty ourselves of our expectations. They are not helpful.

Chapter 8

What Is Clear Time?

'I need you to see me…no judgement, no expectations, just accept me for who I am.'

(Anna, aged 14)

We talk about Clear Time a lot in our work, as it is integral to the 3C Pathway. As a concept, it sounds relatively simple, but in practice it can be challenging.

Clear Time means being **clear of distractions, clear of anxiety** and **clear of expectations** in order to establish secure connections with the autistic children you love, live with or are working with. Autistic children are prone to be on high alert and subconsciously looking for safe people to connect with. We have established why in previous chapters. Feeling isolated, confused and disconnected, either as a cause of autism or as a result of the challenges that autism presents, is a big problem in the development of autistic children. It is through safe, secure connection with others that healthy development happens. It goes without saying that the ability to connect with others is a vital component of a child's development. Connection is reciprocal and for a child to connect with you they must feel safe with you. For autistic children, this feeling of safety is harder to establish, therefore they will need greater help and consideration from you.

A safe person is someone who is able to give their full attention, someone who can be one hundred per cent present with the child, with the intention of actively listening to everything they say and engaging with them on their terms. This means, for example, not looking at a mobile phone while chatting, and not interrupting with additional or non-related communication. It means removing your agenda from that moment and giving them your full attention. It does not necessarily mean eye contact or physical connection, as we know for many autistic children this does not help them to feel connected.

A safe person is a person who manages their own anxiety. Your stress levels, even if not related to anything the child is doing, will have an impact on their ability to connect with you. Autistic children tell us they feel other people's emotions very strongly to a point of physical pain and psychological overwhelm. A feeling of anxiety projected via you can set off alarm bells for the child that indicate to them that you sense danger, therefore they are in danger. In fact, any strong emotions you feel that are not necessarily obvious can trigger feelings of confusion and being overwhelmed in the child.

A safe person is someone who does not have expectations. You don't enter a connected moment expecting a certain outcome, good or bad. The safe person is present in the moment, letting the child lead and being curious as to the outcome. A safe person doesn't judge or presume, does not project disappointment or frustration. Controversially, even positive expectations can be too much pressure, and offering high praise for doing well can lead the child to worry that they can't live up to the standard set.

These states are ideal states for Clear Time.

All young children look externally for their sense of worth and value, but autistic children rely on this even more, so how we relate to them can have a very strong influence on them. Dhriti, parent of six-year-old Aarush, says:

> Giving Aarush time, encouragement and cuddles even though deep down we may be tearing our hair out or running out of time with lots of things to do... We now recognize that we need to go at his pace whatever needs doing, as building a close bond is the most important thing and that means he comes first whatever.

Distractions, anxiety and expectations are very difficult things to minimize. Let's face it, we are often distracted. There are so many things to do in a given day, and when time with any child does not feel productive or fun, we distract ourselves. We might think the child won't even notice, but imagine sitting opposite a friend and they keep furtively glancing at their phone. How valued would you feel in that moment? Autistic children do notice, they sense the disconnect at a deep psychological level that they often can't rationalize.

Keeping your anxiety under control is also hard. If you are the parent of an autistic child, you will have had your fair share of anxious moments. It's not to say that these are not real and valid, but if you try and cover them or let them spill into your Clear Time moments, the time spent with your child will be counterproductive. Taking a few moments to breathe out and check your heart rate before you are with your child makes a huge difference to you, your state, and the ability your child will have to connect with you. It will help them feel safe and less overwhelmed by your energy.

We are told that autistic children can't feel emotions. This is a myth. One young boy told us, when he felt able to, that when he was younger he was 'bluetoothed' to his mum's emotions. He felt what she felt. He felt as if it was in his body. The difference was he couldn't interpret it rationally or tell her at the time. This is a clear example of the autistic challenges of interoception and alexithymia (being unable to define emotions).

It is also hard not to have expectations. We are goal-driven by nature. We like success and progress. It feels good emotionally and offers a feeling of reward and satisfaction. However, it can also put a lot of pressure on you and your child to achieve, achieve, achieve, and leads to disappointment and frustration when you don't 'succeed'.

The sad truth is that for many young people we work with, their young lives often feel like a series of failures and let downs, to themselves and others. All children are hardwired to seek approval and when the indicators are there to suggest they are not being validated – the telling off by a teacher, the rolling of the eyes of a grandparent, the stare of a neighbour, the failed psychological tests, the rejection by their peers or the whispered tones in the house of 'What are we going to do with his child?' – these trigger a belief that they are not worthy, successful or valued. This has a massive impact on their psyche, and from an early age, they will be on high alert for these nuanced responses, which can result in the child avoiding any type of activity for fear of continued disapproval and rejection.

Clear Time is a behaviour, not for the child to adopt but for you to adopt. It's a way of being, a practice that is the antidote to the psychological weight of disapproval, confusion and disconnect that so many autistic people talk about. This is not a way to *'stop'* autism and is not a state of being that is possible to maintain one hundred per cent of the time. It is the way to build a more secure connection in order to start a process of psychological healing, and to build a relationship where fun, friendship, love, nurture and learning can take place. What we are attempting with Clear Time is to create the best environment possible for the child's social, emotional and psychological well-being.

You cannot embark on the 3C Pathway effectively if Clear Time is not understood and regularly practised. The first thing is to notice your energy around your child. Before you engage with your child in Clear Time, clear yourself. Try to approach Clear Time as exactly that, a time where you are not focusing on moving your child forward – you are present, your mind should be clear of your 'to do' list.

Many parents find this difficult to maintain, but we have evidence from both parents and children that it is the ideal state to maintain in order to help the child feel that sense of connection they crave but have always found difficult. It also helps them regain some self-control and feel grounded. As a parent, once you see that this strategy is working for you,

you will feel more confident to do less. On reflection, we feel that Clear Time, in its purest form, is a communication to the child that says, 'I see you; I value you; I want to be with you; I am here, you are safe.'

Clear Time exercises

Here are some examples of Clear Time exercises for you to work on. You will find more at the end of the book.

Our exercises fall into three main categories:

Everyday exercises that are not forced but just happen incidentally while with the child. They are easy to implement, light-touch moments or activities. Some you might do for yourself and some alongside the child.

Proactive exercises that you consciously think about implementing at regular times so the child might be aware that you are working together on something – a conscious shared experience.

Crunch exercises that you work on so that you can support the child when they are having a difficult time.

Everyday Clear Time

- Without the child being made aware, be alongside them in an activity, subtly watching, listening and enjoying them doing what they are doing.
- Your energy and communication should be low and

slow. Let the child lead. Stop if you feel the child is not connecting at all or is getting agitated.

- Start with five minutes daily.

Proactive Clear Time

For you:

- If you are at home, put your phone in another room.
- Go into the kitchen and make yourself a cup of something hot.
- While the kettle is boiling, clear yourself of expectations, distractions and anxiety.
- Watch the kettle boil and do a breathing exercise or the following heartbeat exercise.
- Heartbeat exercise: watch the kettle, place your right hand on your heart and gently tap a resting heartbeat rhythm (approximately 60 beats per minute). You can count in your head as you tap 'and 1 and 2 and 3 and 4', or simply do the rhythmic tapping while breathing slow, deep inhalations and slow, deep exhalations. You will find out what works best for you; remember, this is your personal check in, your time for you.

For your child:

- Set a daily time when the child knows it's your special time to be together doing what they want to do. You can join in, or just be one hundred per cent interested. Be the novice, let them lead. Watch that your enthusiasm levels don't rise too high, as that emotional energy can also be distracting.
- Try to do this for 30 minutes every day.

Crunch Clear Time

- If your child is struggling and is very withdrawn or agitated, your ability to be clear will be tested, but it is now that it is most needed. Avoid the instinct to fuss, fix, judge or get agitated yourself. If you have a good grasp of the Clear Time practice, this is when you need it most.
- Stop, breathe out, still yourself and be totally present with your child. You do not have to be next to them, touching or talking – just be close by in the room, calmly supporting and being there if they need you (see the Honey the dog example in Chapter 1).
- If they are moving about, move with them, but more slowly, and as you do this, tap a heartbeat rhythm on your heart, leg or arm. Mirror them and be completely present. You are checking in to your child. Are they giving you distress signals, elevated energy, stimming or aggression? As you do this, you are validating them; their physiological state is no longer 'wrong' and at the same time you are modelling calmness and acceptance.

Chapter 9

The First C: Connecting

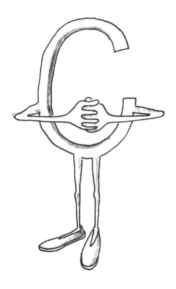

*'Connection for me is when I know someone will not
fix or fuss but accept and understand.'*

(Robbie, aged 10)

Connection is the first step on the 3C Pathway. It is possibly
the hardest, the most fundamental and, if we consider it, the
most obvious step.

What is a connection? What does it signify in human
terms? It is the understanding that we gain from each other

when we spend time in 'joint attention'. It's the feeling people get when they are together in a psychological connection, it is not necessarily a verbal or physical connection.

'I see you, you see me.'

'I get you, you get me.'

'I feel safe in the understanding that you are there for me, that you will keep me safe and I trust you to do that.'

Connection, in this sense, gives you a sense of belonging, a sense of identity and a sense of security. The connection we are talking about is best described as the bond that a parent may have with a child, good friends may have with each other, or even the connection you have with a pet. It's something that not only feels good, but is vital for your cognitive, social and emotional well-being.

The nature of autism and the neurological differences that we have discussed in previous chapters explain what so many of the autistic young people we work with tell us. They say they often feel completely disconnected – disconnected from themselves, from their families, from their peers and from society as a whole.

This is something that most of us can't even imagine, let alone consider experiencing for more than a couple of days. Imagine if you were ill in bed away from your friends, or if you were in a formal setting that you were uncomfortable with, or if you were cut off from social media or in a foreign country and didn't know the language. How would you feel?

We believe that conscious, consistent attempts from you, the parent or professional, at recreating connection is a vital first step in the process of supporting any child to build a healthy relationship with themselves and others. You will model to the child how to connect, and they will learn to connect by the very fact that you are connecting with them. At this point, we are recreating the infant–parent connection that was potentially disrupted in early infancy. You are the teacher of the most fundamental lesson, 'how to feel connected', and you do this by modelling the ideal connective state. If you do not do this, you risk negative physiological, neurological, emotion, sense and muscle memories embedding from an early age.

'I feel disconnected, I can't count on anyone to help, I can't learn' was something that one of our children shared with us.

The foundation stone for social, emotional and cognitive development needs to be *relaid*. In effect, you are taking the child's social learning back to basics and together you are restructuring the neural pathways to understand and recognize what connection feels like.

Once a trusted connection is made with the child, we can then support them to become more self-aware, to understand their autism, to understand human behaviour and understand their own and others' emotions. These are all important steps and should be part of our role. None of this can happen if our children don't feel safe in the initial connection with us as the 'teacher'.

The self-development process starts with them understanding and trusting human connection by experiencing that connection, a true connection with another human being. All children require a secure base for their healthy development, and through connection, you become the secure base.

Your part in this is to make regular connections and make these connections part of your everyday activity.

You can't fake the connection, and it will take patience and willpower on your part to authentically connect. The response to your connection can be slow, and the child may not immediately reciprocate. Remember, your child may have sensory differences that impede their innate ability to enjoy the give-and-take of reciprocal learning. Don't panic or think you must be doing it wrong. If you persist and regularly put connected moments into your daily routine, you will start to see shifts in the connection your child makes with you.

As parents, we too have a need for this connection; it won't just be for the benefit of the child. We crave reciprocity with our child. The reciprocal connection we feel in the responses we get from the children we love or care for is deeply satisfying. We will learn so much from the child in these moments of connection and the relationship becomes more symbiotic. We learn from each other and the bond grows, the understanding grows, and the connection becomes stronger and more valuable.

Connection activities, done alongside, even if the child is not actively joining in with you, are the best way to start.

STEP 1: CONNECT

Everyday connections
Joining
This simple exercise will help with connecting.

- Join your child in what they are doing. If your child is on the computer, be on your computer near them. If your child is running around humming in the garden, run and hum with them.

Validating
This light-touch exercise helps endorse what your child is doing.

- Look for something specific to make a positive comment about, something your child has done in the house or at school or is wearing. Tell them you like it without expectation of any response.

Proactive connections
Mirroring movements
This game helps you join their world.

- Create a game where your child makes a movement that they like, for example spinning or jumping. Copy it, then try it the other way around where you lead and they mirror.

Clear Time
Establish a routine of taking *15 minutes* just for your child. The child should choose an activity. Join in with them but be led by them. This might be a quiet moment. All such moments have value. (See Clear Time exercises from the previous chapter.)

Crunch connections
These exercises reinforce connection and tell your child you're there for them and expect nothing back.

Present and patient
A child in distress will need you to be present. Your energy must be alert but not alarmed. A still hand on their arm or thigh can help, but only if allowed by the child.

Low, slow voice
A child in distress will want you to be near but your energy must be low and your voice pace must be slow.

These connection exercises are a starting point. Once you feel confident with these, you can try some of the exercises at the end of the book. Remember, start slowly using these simple connections and progress to the other exercises once you and your child have created your secure, connected base.

CONNECTION CASE STUDIES

Case study 1: Everyday connection
Cheryl's story
I was starting to feel like it was me. Everyone else in the group was telling everyone how it had moved on, how much progress they'd made by just being with their children and not expecting anything back or anything. Lucy and one of the other parents had tried to reassure me that it was okay, and it was not me [who was at fault] and she didn't mean it, but that made me feel worse. It was week three and although I was pleased about what was happening with people, I was, like I say, thinking 'It's me, what am I doing, not doing, you know?' Then, when I had given up, just when I thought,

'Well, they have told me what to do and I'm doing it,' it happened. My silent boy got my hand and put it on his leg and started to tell me everything that he was doing on **Minecraft**®. Once he started, I was laughing to myself because I didn't think he was ever going to stop... No, seriously, it was amazing, and I was trying so hard not to be over the top, not react too much like I was told, and we just sat there. I couldn't believe it, I was so happy.

Then I realized my shoulders weren't hunched and I wasn't so tense, and it was like a chicken and egg moment.

In Cheryl's case, her need for a result, her expectation, was manifesting in bodily tension and possibly creating a fear in her child that she wanted something from him. When our bodies are tense, they give out more negative energy, and our children, if they have a hypervigilant sensory system, will probably pick up on it. Cheryl's passive connection was what worked in the end.

Case study 2: Proactive connection
Linda's story
I have a natural tendency to always have an expectation about the time I spend with Rachel; umm, yeah, connecting in Clear Time has given us the time to do nothing. Well actually [laughs], it's made me realize I never really just connect and do nothing, because I always have to have a result. I hate it in me and I now realize that needing a result has been part of the problem. I'm always asking, 'How was school? What did you do at break time?', that sort of thing.

It was hard for me to just say something that didn't need an answer, but I started to say things like, 'Your hair looks nice,' or 'Spending time with you is lovely.' I'm aware now that I've probably been making Rachel's anxiety worse as she likes to please me, and often, I realize now, she just can't find the words if I'm asking loads of questions.

I needed to put my needs on the back burner and not think about what the result of the time spent with Rachel might be.

Linda's anxiety was fuelling her and overloading her daughter. She, like many of us, had to help herself to connect without expectations.

Chapter 10

The Second C: Calming

'I can't be calm just because you tell me to! Your anxiety will be catching, like a cold, so if you are calm that is the first step to helping me be calm.'

(George, aged 9)

This is the second step in the 3C Pathway and the one that should be the easiest as it seems so obvious and relatively easy to understand as a concept. Calm suggests the opposite of anxious. A calm physical state, mental state and emotional state is when the body feels relaxed, thinking is not frantic and emotionally we are confident and pragmatic.

A calm or relaxed state has been proven as the optimal condition for any learning to take place. We have explored, in previous chapters, why being calm in the presence of the autistic child is a challenge and why anxiety seems to be such a common state for all. Naturally, someone who is anxious a lot of the time will find it difficult to be calm. Someone who is anxious a lot of the time will also find it difficult to learn.

Chapter 7 on the senses explains why, so often, the autistic child is in chaos and conflict with their surroundings, and how this chaos leads to behaviour that can have a negative impact not only on them getting their needs met, but also on meeting the needs of others around them.

We don't need to rely on scientific research to tell us this, as the children we work with do a great job of explaining it. They tell us that most of the time they feel unsettled and unable to focus, which on its own, without all the daily demands of others, can cause a constant state of physical anxiety and cognitive chaos.

Unfortunately, due to proprioceptive challenges, they can't always adequately interpret the anxiety signals until someone helps them understand what the sensation is, what the cause is and what they can do to have some control over it. Imagine having a feeling in your body that you don't understand, a feeling that also activates many other emotional and physical responses that are equally incomprehensible, and you don't know how to name or control them.

This would undoubtedly be exhausting, and would also regularly get you into trouble with those around you. Many of the so called 'challenging behaviours' that are talked about in relation to autistic children are, we believe, the direct result of the child's anxiety and their inability to deal with this or to get the support they need. Once we help the child understand their anxiety, manage to stay calm ourselves and give them some simple tools to recognize and manage their anxiety, then the 'behaviours' seem to diminish. They can start to understand what calm is and how to achieve it.

When we are anxious, we feel a sense of apprehension in our body based on something happening in our surroundings, an action, a memory, or a sense. It sends a signal to our brain to explore the size, proximity and proportion of the threat:

'Is it a spider that I can ask my friend to remove?'
'Is it a man running towards me with a knife?'
'Is it a memory of a past upset?'
'Is it a bus that is running late so I will miss an appointment?'
'Is it a car that is speeding towards me?'

We feel these anxieties in our body first and then we have an internal assessment/conversation, drawing on past experience and rational thought. We then decide the best action based on how immediate, real or significant the threat is. Take the example of a car heading towards you. This should instinctively lead you to jump out of the way. In terms of a late bus, we may just take a deep breath and accept that we are going to be late.

Whatever the situation, these are strategies that require a lot of internal processing. If processing is a challenge, you will struggle to initially recognize the feeling at a physiological level and then are unlikely to be able to come up with a strategy at a practical level.

The lack of or reduced interoceptive signals in autistic children means they may not even recognize the feeling as anxiety at the point when they could have some control over it and, even if they do, they may not have the cognitive dexterity to work out, in that moment, what it is they need to do to protect themselves.

If you don't trust yourself or others to be able to protect you, this can make you extremely vulnerable and therefore increase the anxiety cycle. It is then that the body's autonomic nervous system does a very wise thing – it decides that it's better to be in a permanent state of alert, ready for any threat of danger. You will probably instinctively revert to the fight, flight or immobilize response. This will be your safety strategy, even if it is not appropriate. The physical and the emotional responses feed each other in a loop. When there is too much of either and the child does not have the capacity to understand, get support or regulate, it can result in mental (psychological) anxiety, which can cause trauma and longer-term associated challenges.

The description above is not necessarily autism, but a consequence of the mental exhaustion that the autistic child feels when not being able to feel connected, calm or able to communicate their needs and wants to others. The Calm step in the 3C Pathway relates to our part in helping the child to understand and reduce their anxiety, and therefore induce a state of calm. This is vital for the child's well-being and their ability to progress.

This is not new thinking; many parents and professionals, with good intentions, believe that the process starts with you getting the child to be calmer. This is the ultimate goal, but we don't start here. Like each step of the 3C Pathway, it doesn't start with the child, but with you. We start by insisting that you, the carer, parent or teacher, need to work on your physical, emotional and mental state before you try and help the child with theirs. Working on your own anxiety first is the best way to help an autistic child be calm.

This is not as easy as it sounds. As parents and carers, we are often anxious without even knowing it. We are working at such a pace, functioning at the speed that society dictates, that we are often operating from an adrenaline-fuelled system. This adrenaline, which may feel normal to you, translates to the autistic child as an unsafe and unsettled person. Even if this isn't obvious to you, it will be a factor in the child's ability to stay connected and trust you to be on their side, supporting them rather than contributing to their feeling of being overwhelmed. Your state can almost 'infect' them, as one child told us, because when the adult they trust is anxious, the security of the child is compromised. The children we work with often tell us that they can 'smell' anxiety in someone, even if they are not in close proximity, which is an interesting observation for children apparently not able to read emotions. We can attempt to understand how they can do this, or we can just accept their word for it, either way, if we start to work on our own state of calm, we can stay connected with them.

Recognizing our own states of anxiety and working on finding moments of calm, we become better placed to help them learn about their anxiety.

It is okay to admit that spending time supporting a child with a different processing system can provoke anxiety. We have not met a parent or teacher yet who has not had anxiety in relation to supporting the child they care for. There is the day-to-day anxiety of witnessing a child in distress or worrying about the tasks and goals that they seem to be missing or 'messing up', and the long-term anxiety of the future and the expected outcomes for the child. This anxiety is normal but will be impacting on your ability to help the child be calm.

Anxiety will feel very normal for an autistic child. Their fear and confusion about the world around them means that they can develop controlling behaviours to help them keep their chaotic feelings in check and bring order to their unsafe world.

It is these behaviours that can also add to the anxiety of the parent or carer. Behaviours that seem antisocial or suggest that the child is not developing at the pace of their peers can be concerning and our instinct is to intervene. We want to fuss or fix. We can feel that if we stop the behaviour, then the child will be less anxious. We need to be honest with ourselves. Are we thinking that if we can stop the behaviour, then we will be less anxious and less worried about the child's future? Do we think that controlling the behaviour will mean that we have a child who is easier to manage, control or teach?

We meet a lot of parents who have little or no support, leaving them isolated and not knowing where to get the best help for their child. Sometimes, working or living with an autistic child can make us anxious as the efforts we make trying to connect and communicate are often thwarted. This leaves us frustrated and tired, and feeling hopeless.

In short, if we don't manage our anxiety sufficiently when relating to a child with autism, it will have a negative effect in all our interactions with them. Their existing state of anxiety will be increased and unintentionally we add to the feelings of confusion, distress, despair and them being overwhelmed.

The calm state is where the best learning happens, and part of the emotional education that we will do in the third step of the 3C Pathway – Communication – is explaining that we have lots of emotions, some that are more productive than others, but all are valid. We then need to guide our child in how to express, regulate and deal with the more challenging ones like anger, sadness, fear and frustration. We can only teach this to our child if we and they are calm.

Calm and relaxed are not permanent states for any human but we need to help our child understand what calm is, what it feels like and to acknowledge the benefit.

STEP 2: CALM

Everyday calm
Personal check-in

- Notice your energy around your child.
  - What makes you anxious?
  - What are your triggers?

Trigger check

- Notice your child's energy and the triggers that disturb them. Sometimes the response is delayed so you may need to be a detective.

Proactive calm
Breathing exercises

- Make breathing exercises a family activity. Talk openly about the effect they can have and model the different ways to do it; for example, blow into the hand or do circle breathing (see the hand trace relaxation exercise in Chapter 13).

Calm spaces

- With your child, design a calm space where they can retreat to and have autonomy. You could use a pop-up tent or a small corner of a room.

Crunch calm
Clear Time

- Once you are both used to Clear Time, allow the child to have Clear Time with you or on their own in their safe space. They can use this time to regulate, reflect and refresh. Model calmness yourself and be aware of your breathing and heart rate.

Low, slow breathing

- When you've been trying out breathing exercises with your child for a while as a proactive activity, you can support them in breathing low and slow when they're really struggling. Be alongside them to give simple instructions, for example, 'I am here, you are safe.' (Use the hand trace relaxation exercise in Chapter 13.)

These calming exercises are a starting point. Once you feel confident with these you can try some of the other exercises at the end of the book. Remember, start slowly using these simple calming strategies and progress to the other exercises once you and your child have created your secure base.

CALMING CASE STUDIES

Case study 1: Proactive calming
Sharon's story

When I was still thinking about the belly breathing, Amira didn't really take much notice but the more instinctive it became for me, the more she connected with me. We never talked about it at all, in fact. I knew it was working when she put her head in my lap and cuddled up to me while we were in Clear Time. She's not normally wanting body contact. If I think about it, who wants to be close to someone who's tense?

Case study 2: Crunch moments
Sandra's story

My instinct, every time my boy had a meltdown, was to try to stop it. I hated seeing his distress, obviously, and I wanted it to stop. I would try to calm him down. I would fuss and talk and try to reassure him. It's instinct, isn't it? One day my partner was so tired when he came in from work that he just flopped down on the sofa. He didn't help me out as I tried to calm my son. I was tired too and a bit annoyed that it appeared he was just leaving it to me. As I made my way into the kitchen, I was aware that his cries were getting quieter – something that never usually happened that quickly. When I went back into the room, my partner and our boy were gently rocking on the sofa. We discussed it later and my partner admitted that he was exhausted and had just sat and rocked and ignored our son. He said he hadn't got the energy to get frustrated. I now understand a bit more how my energy was not helping. I also thought, 'I'm going to do this as well when I can!'

Chapter 11

The Third C: Communicating

'Sometimes I don't understand your words. I just hear your tune. I decide how you are feeling by the tune you are speaking. If I don't like it, I can't reply.'

(Luca, aged 12)

Communication is the third step in the 3C Pathway and is the one that most parents and teachers want to improve as soon as possible. It is seen as the gateway to all social, emotional and cognitive development. We constantly hear:

'My child is not listening to my instructions.'
'Why won't he tell me what he wants?'
'She just won't talk to us.'

As therapists, teachers and parents, we actively encourage communication with the child, but first we must examine our understanding and expectations of communication. Autism is defined as a communication disorder for children with and without spoken language, so it goes without saying that there will be challenges for both parties in this area. As teachers and parents, we instinctively want to go head-on and fix it.

'If only she could tell me what she needs, I could help her.'

Our experience tells us that this is not as simple as just 'fixing it' or 'getting them to talk'. Trying to initiate the relationship with your autistic child at the 'talking part' of the communication process does not always produce the best results. Remember that communication is so much more than just speaking.

Communication is inherently *social*; it's not something you can do on your own. This is where social communication starts, not by talking, but by connecting, using no words, just an exploratory, non-judgemental gaze where the baby and the caregiver lean into each other's rhythms. From the early babbles and smiles, the trust, patience and understanding of the communication process develops via this connection.

This is why we are insistent that our 3C Pathway starts at the Connection step rather than the Communication step.

At the Connection step of the 3C Pathway, we are aiming to mirror and create the optimum conditions for the communication process to be initiated — a back-and-forth reciprocal connection that allows for mirroring and mapping. Our communication skills then develop in the context of a few other important elements: our environment, our family, our cultural setting, and also our neurological maturity.

Humans are innate communicators and autistic children are no different. We all want to communicate, need to communicate and have the ability to communicate. This is good news for autistic children. We have not met an autistic child who cannot communicate. So, what is the challenge?

Is it that the autistic child has a communication disorder or is it merely a communication difference that, in the context of society's expectations, just doesn't match up? Could the child's communication standards not match these expectations because some of the intricate steps required in becoming a competent social communicator are being missed or muddled in early infancy?

Could it be that the learning environment for the child is so chaotic and confusing that they shut down or lose focus, so that fundamental innate learning can't take place, due to their hyper- or hyposensitivity, and subsequent overload — referenced in earlier chapters. In Chapter 10 on calming, we explored how difficult it is for anyone to learn in chaos and confusion.

It's like chicken and egg. Which came first? The communication difference because of the brain wiring, which then causes the child to be anxious, or the recognized levels of anxiety, and the overactive heartbeat that autistic children experience that disable the cognitive functioning required for effective communication?

Could it be that, for an autistic child at the initial developmental stage of social communication, their neurology was not mature enough or ordered enough to lay down the foundations for reciprocity with another human being? In order to learn to communicate, and to develop communication skills, we need to make a connection with the people and the world around us, which for autistic children can be difficult to read or too overwhelming to interpret.

There are two main communication challenges. First, the manner or mode of communication may not be what is expected by family, school or peers. Society expects people to communicate in a certain way. When children learn language, from the outset they are under scrutiny, from school and home. We don't always intend to, but we have expectations. We tend to measure communication progress against other members in the family or judge it as a sign of early intelligence. More importantly, we see good communication skills as a sign of social dexterity. Comments made about typical children might include:

'He gets on so well with his little friends.'
'He is so polite. He always says please and thank you.'
'She chats away for hours and has so many words. She is so clever.'

Health visitors and schools mark communication competency as a milestone for 'healthy/normal' development, and alarm bells are set off if your child is not developing at the same pace or as consistently as their peers.

Socially, communication is a currency used to expand teen and adult life. It impacts on the ability to make friends, keep friends and multiply these friends into friendship circles and groups. This is highly valued in our society and we are judged by our ability to do this well. Not being able to do this 'well' is deemed a failure. As social animals, we don't want to associate with someone who 'can't socialize like us'. This can possibly isolate children and limit their potential to build their social communication skills.

We notice that autistic children, if they do speak, are likely to have a different language style and development profile. They are often very literal, they can often use more adult language and do not see the value in saying please and thank you, or of talking about topics that hold no interest for them. Sarcasm, idioms and metaphors are not easily understood. Autistic individuals may mimic and copy phrases from films, TV shows or other children and adults (echolalia). Their tone and intonation can often seem forced or flat. Turn-taking and the social dance of communication is not adhered to or innately understood.

There are expectations in every communication transaction right from the start, and these expectations get more complicated and challenging as a child develops. A child will learn to communicate in the context of feeling confident around other people who will communicate with them.

Autistic children find it hard to meet these expectations. Without the essential understanding and support of the parent or caregiver, there may be a profound impact on their confidence and ability to communicate going forward. This can lead to social rejection, isolation, frustration at being misunderstood or a feeling of not being heard or of being misrepresented.

The second challenge is the anxiety and stress that we know many autistic children struggle with. Anxiety will undoubtedly impact the ability to use language and produce appropriate responses. You may have very good communication skills but think of a time when you have been very anxious, and someone has asked you, 'What do you need?' and you can't find the words, or if under extreme stress you call someone the wrong name or get muddled in your thinking. Imagine if this happened all the time. You would undoubtedly start to lose confidence in your own ability to form words and connect with others via this form of communication.

Not only would you get left behind in that moment, but it would also hamper you going forward. All your peers are developing along a similar trajectory, learning communication from the very act of being in a shared communication dynamic with each other. In effect, you have been locked out of the game. The game where there are no written rules, but everyone else seems to know how to play. Imagine how you would feel. Isolated, confused, frustrated and aggravated. How might you communicate that? How would you feel if everyone knew the rules to a game and you were expected to play 'nicely', and when you got the rules wrong you were rejected and ridiculed and left out?

Communication is complex, but the good news is that autistic children are resilient and are driven to communicate in order to survive. What we notice is that the child may find their own unique way of communicating. They may use unique sounds, movements or actions, or copy what they see literally without having the ability to interpret the more complicated nuanced elements of communication. Consequently, it can be complicated for those around them to make sense of their communication, and so they then find it hard to connect.

We often read that it is hard to understand the autistic child's communication and that they have a communication problem. But consider this: we too have a problem in understanding and communicating with them. Be aware that it's a two-way street and maybe, as the more confident, competent communicators in the transaction, we need to be the ones to alter our communication to help them to understand us.

There are two main elements in supporting your child at the Communication step. The first is how *you* communicate with them, and the second is how you enable *them* to communicate with you. Both are important because without these two elements, how do either of you share your basic needs, wants and intentions?

A child who cannot communicate their needs and wants will react in two extreme ways – frustration or despair. The frustration can present as angry, aggressive and destructive behaviour, and the despair can look like shutting down, being upset and crying.

Think of the toddler who is demanding something, but the adult can't understand what they want. Frustration and despair are obvious, but that toddler will gradually develop spoken words, patience and appropriate ways to communicate with others to get their needs understood and met.

What we do know is that when the child is calm and trusts the person they are with, and there is a communication system that is shared, then reciprocal communication can happen. It may be communication without words, using body language, gestures and signs.

It is vital to remember that step 3, Communication, comes after steps 1 and 2. After you have connected and are calm. However, you may well see communication automatically improving and becoming more reciprocal as a natural consequence of the step 1 Connection and step 2 Calm.

STEP 3: COMMUNICATION EXERCISES

Everyday communication
Talk their talk

- If your child has a unique way of expressing themselves, acknowledge it by using it with them. It might be sounds, actions, art, breathing, writing or reading.

Quality listening

- Listen more than you talk. When your child shares, listen without judgement and don't push for more information.

Proactive communication
Lists and pics

- Create a system in the house with your child that allows them to share their needs, practical and emotional. This could be picture boards, mood boards and emoji pics around the house. Make communication less complicated so that needs get met and understanding is clear.

Clear Time

- Use Clear Time to allow the child to share infor-mation that is important to them. It may be facts about something they love, or something confusing about feelings and people. It may be how they want to be supported when feeling overwhelmed. Listen with interest and love.

Crunch communication
Say everything by saying nothing

- It will not help to add verbal stimulus to an already overwhelmed child. Saying nothing might seem counterintuitive, but remember, just being with them is communicating support and understanding.

Low, slow commands

- When you have established what your child needs when feeling overwhelmed, you can remind them in a low, slow tone; for example, 'Go to your safe place and listen to music,' or, 'Breathe into your hand.' A child can forget their strategies when in meltdown. This will increase their out-of-control feeling. Model their strategies or remind them of their strategies in a low, slow tone. This will give them the power to self-regulate.

COMMUNICATION CASE STUDIES

Case study 1: Everyday communication
Janice's story
It took me forever to stop pushing my agenda, probably because I wasn't even aware how quick my tempo is...

I think, no actually I know, that I was a nightmare, but I didn't know it then, and I still can't do it naturally, but I have slowed down around Amy. One thing I do is, if I come in the room and want to say something, if she seems at all agitated, I walk out again breathing as I go and then turn round and come back in. It works for me and even makes me giggle sometimes as I see myself doing it. Laughter gets me through, when I can!

Case study 2: Crunch communication (meltdown or shutdown)
Tony's story

I'd been to that many interviews, it wasn't funny, and they all merged into one big 'You're useless.' I'd get there and practise my breathing and try to visualize getting the job and then when we were called in to do some practical work I just couldn't do it. I couldn't understand what the instructions were; it was just like listening to jangly rubbish white noise with bells and screeches. I would sit there and think, 'Well, do something,' and so I would, and I'd be right off-task. It was...humiliating and I got to the point where I would rather have my mum moan and worry at me *again*, than leave the house. I really wanted a job, but it didn't seem very probable; actually, it wasn't going to happen. I stopped bothering about washing and I just was...off. It wasn't until I realized that when someone gave me instructions, I just *could not* listen to it all at once – especially when I was anxious, like in an interview.

When Tony's next interview arrived, he made it into the interview room. Only this time he had a translator/mentor who used heartbeat 'parcels of communication' to explain to him what he had to do. He didn't get that job, but because his confidence was improving, he eventually secured employment.

Once you have created a secure base for communication, we then encourage you to build a system of communication with your child where you can teach them about emotions, and they can talk about their concerns and confusions.

There are lots of communication strategies in Chapter 14, but start slowly and wait until you are confident to move on to more complex activities and strategies.

Chapter 12

Why Is the Heartbeat So Important for the 3C Pathway and Clear Time?

'When I felt his heartbeat, it was pounding even when he appeared calm. I realized how hard his body must be working all the time; it was like his system was working overtime.'

(Simon, parent)

Some of our most significant testimony for our **heartbeat** exercises and **beat to beat** work has come from parents and teachers who have embraced the approach. One parent was having a really hard time leaving her eight-year-old son Nat at the school gate. Angela was anxious and emotional, and Nat's anxiety was sky high. Angela was convinced he was in danger of becoming a 'school refuser'. She had become so anxious that she dreaded every school morning and life was quickly spiralling out of control. Some mornings they were hours late to the school gate. Even when they finally arrived, it had got to the point where he would only go into the class if she stayed at school. The school staff were really understanding and suggested she sat in the corridor outside the classroom to help keep him in school. It was a situation that was not sustainable.

It was at this point that we met Angela at our Parent Autism Awareness Training. We start our workshops with introductions and parents share their most pressing concerns. This mum shared her anxiety about school. Others in the group nodded and, as might be expected, we weren't surprised by her story as so many of us have been there, or experienced similar situations.

Three weeks later and three weeks of Angela spending Clear Time mirroring Nat and using heartbeat and beat to beat exercises, this was her account at the beginning of our third workshop:

> The heartbeat hug has been a game changer for us. The constant rhythmic tap really seems to soothe my little boy's anxieties, especially when waiting for the gate to open at school in the morning. It helps bring him right down and he's going in on his own, I couldn't believe it the first time I used it in the morning.

We had been doing it together in Clear Time, which he was really enjoying, and I just did it without thinking and he did it back and then turned and walked in... I was shocked and then so relieved, but I tried to stay calm and waved.

Later in this chapter, we will set out the reasons why this simple connection worked so effectively.

Sadly, the situation this mum found herself in is all too common. She was constantly feeling anxious and exhausted and couldn't see a way forward. Sometimes, we don't realize just how anxious we are. It doesn't matter what it is that is worrying us, whether it's finishing a task, getting out of the house or getting our children to eat some breakfast, often we are anxiously rooted in our expectations. Either we desperately want to get things done, or we feel there is no way anything is going to improve. Both are expectations.

Autistic children tell us that they feel and sense other people's anxiety at a deep level, maybe deeper than we can even imagine. They might not understand it, but they sense it like a bad smell. If you, as a parent or caregiver, are anxious, even if you are consciously trying to cover it when with your child, they will feel your anxiety and their heartbeat will rise. This elevation in heart rate will trigger concern and confusion and even if they are not conscious of why their body state is changing, they will have an automatic response. This is known as the fight, flight or immobilize response. Physiologically, our autistic children's interoception – the sense that informs them about their internal bodily sensations, such as the pounding of their heart, the flutter of butterflies in their stomach, or the feeling of hunger – often does not work as efficiently.

As discussed earlier, our feelings, thoughts and perceptions are also influenced by the interaction between our body and our brain. Knowing this shows us why it can be very hard for our children to circumnavigate their anxiety and ours, and why their heart rate can become elevated.

When your child is anxious, among their other bodily changes, an enormous amount of adrenaline will be released. Their increased heart rate will pump the blood to their muscles to activate the fight, flight or immobilize response.

Not being able to understand bodily signals and not being able to cognitively unravel why changes are happening disables the child. They cannot take the necessary action to reduce the adrenaline flow. Often you will witness extreme examples of this response – a child runs away, withdraws, acts out aggressively or becomes immobile. These are all instinctive responses to an oversupply of adrenaline.

If you are the cause or accelerator of the increased adrenaline, by being anxious in their presence, it becomes increasingly difficult for them to manage this appropriately. This might result in you becoming the 'enemy' in that moment. You become an additional sensory overload, and once they are anxious, any form of meaningful connection will be harder to make. As a result, it is likely that the anxiety will spiral in both you and your child.

Every second of every day, our hearts are having electrical conversations with our brain. Our heart tells our brain what kind of energy to send to the body, so the heart is doing a lot more than keeping us alive when it beats.

If you sense danger, it's your heart that will give you the first signal. It will pound and it will then send a signal to your brain that says, 'We need the kind of energy that can help us run or fight or make us invisible,' and then the brain decides what action to take.

Research tells us that all babies are born with an elevated heart rate, which begins to slow down at the age of about six years. Another interesting fact is that our heartbeats are not regular. In fact, as we breathe in our heart rate increases in pace and as we breathe out our heart rate decreases in pace. This is also why, when we exhale with a good deep breath, we can feel more relaxed and calmer, and when we take a big breath in, we can feel more fired up and ready for action. In autistic children, there have been two noticeable differences detected. One is that the heartbeat does not decrease at the same age as a typical child. The other is that the differences others experience in the inhalation and exhalation of breath are muted in autistic children.

If autistic children have a higher resting heart rate than their developing peer group, and autistic children have a different breathing pattern, it can mean that some internal responses (interoception, for example) activated by breathing rhythms are not happening unconsciously or as efficiently.

This higher resting heart rate experienced by autistic children could account for some of the challenges associated with autism, predominantly anxiety – the autonomic nervous system, which none of us has any control over, will be working in overdrive most of the time. This is not only exhausting but potentially terrifying and the child will sense danger everywhere. If they don't understand at a cognitive or psychological level why they are responding differently to their peers, this can also be extremely distressing. How many times, if they *can* articulate it, have we heard our children say, 'I just want to be like other people'?

Although we tend to be more aware of our breathing than our heartbeat, perhaps it's time to 'tune in' to our heartbeats and help them to help us.

The heartbeat is the first job that an embryo performs. That heartbeat also produces a 'primal symbiotic interdependence' in mother and child – in other words, it is a *connection* between two humans. We suggest that this pure heartbeat function can comfort and aid communication through the muscle and sense memory of being in the womb. All our memories come from, among other things, what we experience through our senses.

The effect of sharing breathing rhythms is known to take people back to a secure place deep in their unconscious memory. This is also the place where the mother and the child's hearts were beating as one. For some autistic children, this was the first and the last place they may have felt totally secure. They were uncluttered with the additional sensory and environmental stimuli that they find so hard to translate into meaningful physiological and psychological messages.

If we keep repeating, through tapping, a simple resting heartbeat rhythm (about 60 beats per minute), eventually our body will recognize it as *calming*. Our bodies can acquire a new, physically calmer, muscle sense and, eventually, emotional memory.

By practising heartbeat exercises we can become calmer, and then through modelling calmness, using heartbeat exercises, we can start to connect calmly.

To us, it made sense to explore using this unilateral leveller to *calm* ourselves and affect our breathing – practising making it slower and slower. To us, it also made sense to use that rhythm to *connect* with our autistic children.

The heartbeat can help to make a connection with our children that doesn't make them feel as if they are falling short of our expectations. In our experience, when the pressure is taken off and their body – and your body – is calm, they will exceed anyone's expectations!

In our chapter on communication we talked about the importance of *connecting calmly* before we *communicate* our wants. The rhythm of the heartbeat can also be used very successfully in verbal communication once we are calmly connected.

An autistic adult told us that when people speak to him, if he is anxious and experiencing sensory overload, he 'hears all the ups and downs of the voice and how loud or how soft the person is speaking, but he can't make sense of what is being said'.

It's hard to reply to someone or interact when you haven't noticed non-verbal cues like facial expressions, and you haven't heard the instructions, because all you've heard is noise. If we simplify the way we say things and support our communication using the heartbeat rhythm, that we all instinctively understand and feel comforted by, in our experience it aids communication.

Shakespeare wrote his verse in a rhythm called iambic pentameter and the rhythm of the iambic pentameter mimics the human heartbeat. Shakespeare's actors had very little time to learn their parts, so the rhythmic pulse of the heartbeat helped them to memorize their lines, and to hear where they were supposed to speak. Feeling the heartbeat rhythm helped the actor move the play forward with a certainty that we all subliminally recognize as the rhythm of life: the heartbeat.

We don't suggest you introduce your child to Shakespeare, but if you speak or sing simple nursery rhymes, you may notice that some are also written in a heartbeat rhythm. There are, however, many different verse rhythms, but arguably the iambic heartbeat rhythm is the easiest to pick up.

You can use nursery rhymes as a way of creating heartbeat rhythms in your speech, speaking them to your child and, with your child, changing pace but keeping the heartbeat rhythm. The rhythmic nursery rhymes that we learn so easily when young are one of the things that helps us discover words and remember them. We also find these rhymes comforting, as they often act as the glue in childhood social situations.

We have been amazed at the effect the heartbeat rhythm can have, and how it supports the 3C Pathway. At the Connect step, it will give you simple rhythms to share. At the Calm step, it is soothing to take the rhythm low and slow, as in a lullaby. At the Communication step, try to adjust your speech patterns to be in line with a heartbeat rhythm. You will notice the heartbeat rhythm forces you to slow down, have a more consistent pace, limit your vocal range and cadence (the up and down of the voice) and minimize your words. This can be both clarifying and calming for the child you are trying to connect with.

But we are getting ahead of ourselves. Before we look at improvements in verbal communication skills using the heart-beat rhythm, we must stress the importance of the heartbeat when first used as a connecting intervention where you have no expectations.

Throughout this book, we come back to the importance of us, as parents, emptying ourselves of anxiety, emptying ourselves of distractions and emptying ourselves of expectations. *It is possibly one of the hardest things to do*, but if we try and imagine how hard it is for autistic children to meet people's expectations, when their bodies are wired, and they feel like running away and hiding, it is easy to understand why regulating our heart rate can help. When our autistic children are in distress and lash out to stop people's demands, or zone out completely, we can start to understand that it might feel better for that child if they can de-escalate their body before they try to meet our expectations.

No one can function well if demands are made on them when they feel anxious, and their body feels 'jangly'. We must also bear in mind that some of our children can't physically or emotionally connect with the feelings they are having and that must be frightening, especially if someone then says, 'I need you to...'. We really want to encourage you to look at the heartbeat as a powerful way to initiate, support and sustain each step in the 3C Pathway.

It is also important to point out that all these heartbeat exercises should not be taught while the child is anxious or in distress.

Heartbeat rhythms should be shared in a fun way and should be done at an age-appropriate level. Normalize the exercises by encouraging all the family to participate and learn something new. Make the exercises part of the daily routine and stick to the routine if possible.

Feeling connected is a powerful benefit of a calm, regular heartbeat rhythm. If we are in rhythm with other people, and our hearts are beating at the same slow, calm rate, the effect is very powerful. The effect is not just physiological, through the calming effect of exhalation and regular heartbeat, but psychological.

This is one of our principal heartbeat exercises that can be incorporated into each step of the 3C Pathway. This is a great way of keeping in touch with your energy and the energy of your child.

HEARTBEAT HUG

Connection – create a shared rhythm.

Calming – bring down your heart rate and theirs.

Communication – talk in the rhythm of the heartbeat and also talk about the heartbeat and explore it together.

● Hug your child and softly tap a heartbeat on their back (some children love this, some don't – as with all the exercises it is not a one size fits all). Experiment with hugs or other ways of sharing the heartbeat rhythms. Tap on their arm or leg. Use a pillow, tap on a surface, beat a drum. Eventually, if it seems appropriate, share with your child the reason why you are doing heartbeat rhythms. For example, 'I feel calmer when I do this.' 'I was feeling anxious, so I am doing this.' Remember we are not 'doing to' or strategizing, we are modelling calm, leaning in and tuning in to the child's communications.

CASE STUDIES ON THE IMPORTANCE OF HEARTBEAT

Case study 1: Proactive connection

'I didn't realize how anxious I was about her maths!'

Maths homework was a regular point of contention and stress in Hannah's household for both her and her daughter, Daisy. Some weeks they would sit together in front of it for hours, but still nothing would get done.

Hannah would spend a significant amount of time encouraging Daisy to do her maths homework but there was so much struggle involved.

Hannah would try not to shout at Daisy or tell her off. She would try to encourage her and give her goals and incentives to get it done, but she was always willing Daisy to get it done, even if she didn't verbally communicate this. She was, however, non-verbally communicating her own need for the homework to get done. Although Hannah's energy was fast-paced and jangly, Daisy still wanted her mum to be alongside her while she did her homework. Hannah had suggested to Daisy that it might be easier for her to concentrate on her homework on her own. This suggestion had resulted in an outburst and eventual meltdown from Daisy, which Hannah later unpicked to discover why.

Hannah did not try to reason with Daisy when Daisy was in distress. Instead, she waited until they were sitting side by side in the car on the way to school the next day before mentioning the incident about the maths homework. Daisy was still adamant that her mum be with her while she did her homework. The conversation seemed to just go around in circles (something that we, as parents, can probably identify with).

Hannah continued struggling to deal with her daughter's maths homework, so things stayed the same as most approaches to change things would result in a meltdown. Nevertheless, in one of our workshops, Hannah shared with the group how she and her daughter had finally reached a breakthrough in what used to be a stressful activity. It wasn't until Hannah explored her own feelings towards the situation that shifts started to happen.

Hannah's story

I sat down next to Daisy as usual and this time I thought, 'Don't say anything, just be here, like Tessa and Jane said,' but three-quarters of an hour in, Daisy still hadn't started. I suddenly thought – do the heartbeat tapping, although I was worrying that it would seem that I was again doing something to get her to do what I wanted... But umm, it was like it helped calm me as well as my daughter, it was like a real lightbulb moment for me and Daisy. It usually took an hour-and-a-half on average to do her maths homework and this time we sat down and I used the heartbeat and it took us ten minutes!

She didn't even know I was doing it, but it calmed me! I stopped giving her grief. I stopped being anxious about what was going to get done and she seemed to relax. I think I took the fear away. She's always worried about what I expect or getting it wrong – yeah, I think it just took the fear away for both of us. Previously, I didn't realize how anxious I was about her maths.

The last statement could be related to anything. In Hannah's case, it was maths homework. It sounds so familiar, doesn't it? Hannah's experience with Daisy's homework highlights how our children can often sense our anxiety, which can then be reflected in their behaviour.

Case study 2: Proactive communication

> 'It's amazing for helping them to calm and now they're independently asking for heartbeat time to regulate themselves.'

Anna is a teacher who had attended a conference where we had demonstrated some of our heartbeat work. Anna is clearly a dedicated and empathetic teacher who really tries to be, in her words, 'the best teacher I can' but she also told us she had been finding mornings at school really challenging. Her class had one-to-one support in most cases, but mornings were still chaotic. She teaches in a special school and has a class of eight children.

We met her six months later at another conference where she told us about her use of heartbeat rhythms.

Anna's story

I've been using heartbeat therapy with the children in my school for about five months now. I've found that it's amazing for helping them to calm and now they're independently asking for heartbeat therapy to regulate themselves... It's really beautiful and it works. We do three sets of heartbeat tapping and then three sets of breathing exercises. Then we do the exercise where you breathe in through the nose, and then as you breathe out through the mouth you press on the heart to slow down the heart rate. Some of my kids aren't comfortable doing it on their heart so I've told them they can do it on their leg or wherever they want to do this. And then we have mindful choosing, so they can choose either heartbeat, breathing exercises or massage. For instance, if they choose massage, they make a massage train, one behind the other, and use heartbeat tapping on each other as well. We do it every day in the morning and before maths. It's a subject that scares them, so we bring them down first so they're nice and calm.

We thought we would include Anna's testimony as it illustrates her Clear Time approach. She leaned in with no goals. Modelling calm has really helped her practice, and her children's well-being. The fact that her children were finding it hard to transition from home to class was obvious to her, but she told us she hadn't realized how much her anxiety had impacted on them.

She has been creative, present and led by the children's need to regulate themselves. By leaning into the behaviours of her class and aiding them to work with the signals their bodies were giving them, she gave them autonomy. The compassionate subliminal messages they were now experiencing meant that she 'saw' them, rather than starting the day by strategizing them. She also told us, 'We get much more done now, and I suppose it's probably because we are all so much more chilled, me and the learning support assistants. It's also fun and they keep coming up with new ways to do it.'

Chapter 13

The Role of Drama Exercises in Our Work

'The body in motion evokes a kinesthetic empathetic understanding on the part of the participants and embedded knowledge can take place.'

(Reynolds and Reason 2012, pp.30–31)

We use drama exercises throughout our work. Many of them appear in the 3C Pathway. We also use them in our professional workshops to help the participants to 'walk in the shoes' of the children they love, live and work with.

They are the foundation of our work in our drama sessions and collaborative improvisations that help us to create our films. Ultimately, as playful activities, they help us all to explore communication, verbally, non-verbally, physically, cognitively and emotionally.

This chapter is separated into two sections, the first being the exercises we use in our workshops, and the second the exercises we use in our drama settings. We hope that you can explore and discover the joy of drama and its flexibility as a form of expression. You can play, have fun and even create your own exercises.

We do this in our workshops via drama exercises that have been designed to give parents, carers and staff an idea of what it might feel like to be autistic. Clearly, it is impossible for a non-autistic person to fully experience what it is like to be autistic and every autistic individual is different, so not all experience the world and interactions in the same way. We design our exercises to create sensory overwhelm and cognitive chaos, based on what the young people we work with tell us. The experience our participants feel during the exercises is a representation. The exercises have been created from our personal knowledge and professional experiences of being with and communicating with autistic children and young people. They have also been trialled with autistic students, and their collaboration and feedback have helped in further development of the exercises.

As actors and drama teachers we are always committed to engaging the audience and bringing stories to life. We bring this same commitment into our parent and professional workshops. We know that to keep an audience engaged you need to make learning interactive, but more than that, to really understand autism we believe you need to gain a sense of lived experience. You can do this intellectually by reading and learning from the accounts of autistic people and ploughing through the scientific and medical journals, which we have done, but what we do in addition is to use kinesthetic empathy as the main learning tool in our workshops. This means understanding something through your whole body.

In our workshops, we find it helps parents and carers to understand autism at a deeper level, before we move on to things they can do to help. We need to understand, through our senses and our bodies, because our senses create our emotional memories. Ultimately, we need our emotional memories to be able to empathize. As parents, we are keen to connect so that we can learn as much as we can about what makes our children tick. Being understood is what any of us want, autistic or not.

If you just use your 'thinking self', you will always be looking in on your child's behaviour and intellectually trying to unravel it, rather than leaning in to the behaviour through empathetic connection. This way of connecting validates the child.

Research suggests that there are several types of empathy – cognitive, moral, perceptual and emotional. All have in common the need to relate to another being or object. Kinesthetic empathy is about the person doing the exercise, experiencing and learning about emotions (their own and others') and cognition (their own and others'). It's the process of understanding another person's perspective.

In essence, what we are doing is using interactive exercises that help participants to feel what cognitive chaos, anxiety and the processing of confusion are like. We then show, as a consequence of these things, how difficult it is to express accurately what you feel and need. Parents, teaching and healthcare professionals then begin to understand how hard it is for the child or pupil to communicate how they feel, what their needs are or the distress they are in. When the participants have felt it, they have a route to kinesthetic empathy. A parent of one workshop participant says:

> We had never really been able to understand and appreciate what it means to become overloaded, so it gave us a great insight into how our child might feel and why they react in the way that they do. It was so good to actually experience sensory overload myself; it was horrible and stressed me out, I felt hot and angry and I wanted it to stop.

Workshop exercises

The following exercises work from the 'outside in' by creating physical difference from an outside stimulus. If someone says 'jump' and you jump, it is an outside stimulus (someone telling you to do it) that has changed your energy. You jump, and your pulse and heart rate will increase. If you try to mirror someone, it will require you to use all your senses to create the physical movements. We need to be able to empathize with the cognitive chaos caused by both internal and external overstimulation. We also need to understand that physical reciprocity is vital for learning. Researchers additionally suggest that interactional synchrony and reciprocal give-and-take play a vital part in the development of empathy, self-regulation and symbol use. Studies have also revealed that repeated reciprocal gestures can help build organizational skills.

RECIPROCITY EXERCISE

Mirroring

This exercise looks at developing a mutual understanding with each other. It requires two people.

- Decide who is person A and who is person B.
- Stand opposite each other at an arm's length.
- Person A makes small arm movements and person B mirrors/copies the movements as accurately as possible. Try to be as synchronized as you can, so person A should not do the movements too fast or make them too complicated.

How did that feel? Did it feel more satisfying when you were synchronized?

- Now person B leads, and you repeat the same exercise.

Were you able to follow each other more easily now that you have tuned into each other's energy?

- Repeat the exercise, only this time there is no leader. You simply mirror each other. Ideally, you shouldn't be able to see who is leading – it should look totally synchronized.

How did that feel? How did you do it?

- Did anybody say, 'you first' or nod that it was their turn? Did you read each other? Was there reciprocal give-and-take?
- Now person B stands on one leg and closes one eye.

You now have two sensory differences. Do the exercise again with person A leading, and this time person A goes just a little faster and makes the movements a little more complicated.

How did that make person B feel? Where in your body did you feel tension (in your neck or head)? What would you have done if you had to continue with the exercise for an hour? How did that make person B feel? Was there frustration with person B that time?

- Person A may have adjusted their movements (slowed down and simplified movements) to help person B. This demonstrates person A being empathetic. However, person A could see person B's challenges.

What if person B's challenges were not visible? Would person A have been so empathetic?
If we change our energy and slow down our communication, we are taking some of 'the noise' out of the interaction and making it easier for person B to reciprocate. This leads to person B feeling validated, which in turn builds confidence.

One parent reported that while subtly mirroring her daughter's movements she noticed that her daughter became less frenetic and agitated. The mum had created a mirroring game. When her daughter bounced onto the sofa, she also slowly bounced onto the sofa. Her daughter started to bounce while sitting. Her mum bounced gently with her and eventually 'the tsunami of energy that is my daughter' (to use her mum's words) started to self-regulate. It was not a cognitive choice that the girl had made. Her body had tuned in to her mum. Energy is a great thing, but it can, if not understood and regulated, quickly turn into energy that can drive the mind and body to an unhelpful place. We then witness distress signals, as the person starts to feel out of control.

COGNITIVE CHAOS EXERCISE

This simple exercise, carried out in a controlled, safe environment, creates what we call 'cognitive chaos' or not being able to think straight. Using your imagination and your muscle, emotion and sense memory, you will 'walk in their shoes'. You will feel it physically, but the exercise *will* end. Our children don't have the luxury of knowing it is going to stop at some point.

You will need three people but if there are only two of you, you can record the instructions on a smartphone.

Jump – Clap – Up – Down – Stop – Go

- Remember these instructions:
  - *jump* means *clap*
  - *clap* means *jump*
  - *up* means *bend your knees*
  - *down* means *put your arms in the air*
  - *stop* means *run on the spot*
  - *go* means *stand still.*
- One person gives the instruction in any order of jump, clap, up, down, stop, go (or use your recording).
- One person asks simple questions like, 'What day is it?', 'What did you have for breakfast?'.
- Start slowly, then build the speed, continue asking the questions. Participants must keep doing the

physical movements at the same time as answering the questions.

- If you want to make it even harder, get the participants to run on the spot, to get their heart rates up, before they start the movements. This simulates an approximation of what it must feel like to have a system that is 'a little bit twitchy'.
- Have fun!

If you do the exercise as a participant, you will experience a 'motor action' (clapping/jumping, etc.) that influences your affective state (heart rate/breathing). As you try to answer the questions you will probably feel anxiety. This stimulates the primal instinct of fight or flight. Now reflect on what it must feel like for your child as they try to keep up while not being able to understand and follow the instructions or express how that makes them feel.

Parents often use this simple exercise for raising awareness with their extended family. A father described the result as incredible, not for him directly but the impact it had on his child's grandad who refused to acknowledge the child's autism, even though there had been a diagnosis.

TRUST EXERCISE

The autistic body often finds it hard to trust. We know that if you have difficulty trusting the signals that your body gives you, you will find it harder to trust outside stimuli as you are already trying to decipher something that you don't understand.

Think of yourself as an outside stimulus; this will remind you that you may sometimes seem to an autistic child as something to be frightened of. This may be a difficult concept to grasp, as we are their parents or teacher and we are trying to help. Take the personal feelings of rejection that can occur and reframe them with this exercise. You will soon experience an approximation of what it might feel like to find it hard to trust.

The exercise requires at least two people but can be played with up to 20 people. You will need enough room to walk around without bumping into things or other people.

Blind cars

- Get into pairs facing each other at arm's length – one of you is the 'car' and the other is the 'driver'. The car turns their back on the driver.
- The driver puts their hands on the car's shoulders and uses signals to direct the car:
  - *a tap on both shoulders* means *walk*
  - *a tap on the right shoulder* means *turn to the left*
  - *a tap on the left shoulder* means *turn right*
  - *a tap on the top of the head* means *stop*.

The car must close their eyes. This is where the trust comes in!

- Play until the car wants to open their eyes. Have a chat about what that felt like to be trusted or to have to trust.
- Repeat the exercise with the car becoming the driver and the driver becoming the car.
- Now ask:

- Did I feel safe?
- Did I trust myself?
- Did I trust the other person?
- Where in my body did I feel tension?
- Did I enjoy it and, if yes, why?

These questions will elicit different answers from the car and the driver, as the car was putting their trust in the driver, and the driver was experiencing the responsibility of keeping the car safe. Even if the driver doesn't take their responsibilities seriously, learning can take place as you unpick why this is. There are so many learning points in this simple exercise as we rarely put ourselves in the position of taking away one of our senses.

PROCESSING EXERCISE

Making a cake
This exercise requires three people.

- Person A gives the instructions for making a cake.
- Person B mimes making a cake.
- Person C is the 'voice in the head' of person B, the participant making the cake.

The idea of the exercise is to simulate the difficulties encountered if you are a literal thinker who finds it hard to process lots of instructions.

- Person A starts to give instructions, for example:
  - Get a bowl and mixing spoon.
  - Get a bag of flour.
  - Get some butter, sugar and eggs.

- Person B mimes the actions.
- Person C's role, as the 'voice in the head', is to confuse the cake maker. As person A gives the instructions 'Get a bowl', person C listens to what is being said and voices questions like:
  - 'Get? What is get?'
  - 'Where do I get a bowl?'
  - 'What kind of bowl? A bowling ball?'
- Person A must keep giving person B instructions, and person C must keep asking questions.

How long is it before the cake maker gives up? Note how they give up. Do they just stop (immobilize), throw up their arms and laugh or walk away (fight/flight)?

Again, this is a crude approximation of what it might feel like to try to follow instructions when you do not process them in the same way as other people. You will probably experience 'cognitive chaos' as you won't be able to think straight and consequently you won't be able to execute the instructions.

Now reflect on what that might feel like for the child in your care. You are now empathizing. You have felt it. Next time your child stares at you blankly when you give them a string of instructions, or finds it stressful to do things, you will have a much better understanding of the challenges they face.

Solutions will include simplifying your language and bringing your energy down. Try to use a heartbeat rhythm as you speak, and give one instruction at a time. Your communication mode is key. Often those who share our children's lives, but are not the primary caregivers, can find it difficult not to judge 'behaviours' and in turn judge our parenting skills. By 'walking in our children's shoes' they too can gain a much greater understanding of our children's challenges and consequently have a better understanding of why we are 'leaning in' and not immediately trying 'to fix' our children.

SENSORY OVERLOAD EXERCISE

The classroom

The object of this exercise is to create an environment that impacts on the senses and consequently the person's processing potential. We are creating cognitive chaos to create an empathetic connection. The connection won't be forgotten as it will be experienced physically, emotionally and cognitively through the senses, creating muscle, emotion and sense memories.

- For this exercise, you will need:
    - three pairs of cheap glasses with strips of sticky tape on the lenses (leave some gaps so the person wearing them has some sight but feels visually challenged)
    - three chairs
    - three pieces of paper with unintelligible sentences in various fonts
    - two or three objects that you can use to make a noise – a drum or tambourine is great, but a saucepan and a spoon will do the job just as well
    - a plastic bag with something with a strong smell in it
    - a scratchy bath brush
    - five people:
        • three people to play school children
        • one to play teacher

- one to create a 'sensory landscape' using the props.
- Place three chairs in a line approximately half a metre from each other.
- The three people playing the children sit on the chairs and put on the glasses. Hand them the written text.
- The 'teacher' starts the lesson by telling the pupils that they have high expectations and expect the pupils to be able to read the text without faltering.
- The 'teacher' asks pupil 1 to read the text. As pupil 1 tries to read the text, the person creating the sensory landscape starts banging the saucepan, at the same time as wafting the smelly bag under their noses. They could then switch to tickling the back of their necks or gently rocking their chairs. As soon as pupil 1 starts to struggle, the 'teacher' stops and moves to pupil 2 and repeats the exercise. The 'teacher' gives pupil 2 even less of a chance and swiftly moves to pupil 3. All of the time the sensory landscape is being maintained, moving between the pupils. Throughout, the 'teacher' comments on the pupils' efforts, 'I know you can do better', 'Why are you finding this difficult?'
- Continue until one of the pupils 'gives up'. When this happens, the 'teacher' should ask, 'Why have you given up so easily?'
- Consider:
  - How did it make the pupils feel?
  - Where in the pupils' body did they feel tension?
  - What would have helped them complete the task?
- The 'teacher' explains that calming the body and

bringing the energy down can help in accessing learning.
- The 'teacher' models breathing and heartbeat exercises.

Using drama

We have talked about how we use drama in our workshops, but we also use drama as a social activity for autistic children and young people, as part of our drama clubs. We have added some of the exercises we incorporate into our sessions that can be adapted by you to use with your children in a fun, explorative way and to help them learn about self-regulation.

RELAXATION EXERCISE
Negative tension into positive energy

- Sit or stand, face forward, relax your shoulders. Turn your head to the right and look as far as you can, over your shoulder directly behind you. Try to spot something, a picture, a crack in the wall, something that you can take a mental snapshot of, and remember the image. Repeat on the left side.
- Look straight ahead again and visualize the two images. Raise your arms and with the thumb and index finger of each hand take hold of your earlobes.
- Massage your earlobes vigorously. Try to make them tingly and hot. Do this for about 45 seconds.
  - Make sure you are belly breathing (see Chapter 14) and aware of any tension in your shoulders. Release your earlobes and roll your shoulders back.

- Look over your right shoulder and see if you can see further behind you than the object you visualized. Repeat over the left shoulder. You should find that you can turn your head more easily.

This is an exercise that actors often do before going on stage. When we are tense, lactic acid contributes to creating stiffness in our muscles. The massaging of the earlobes evidently helps to bring blood into the head. Lactic acid stops the blood from flowing so easily.

VISUALIZATION EXERCISE

Calming blue green and orange

This exercise works on the simple premise that blue and green are perceived as calming colours and orange as invigorating.

- Either sit or lie down, whichever feels most comfortable or is convenient at the time. Close your eyes and think of the colour blue. Think of an image that makes you feel calm and safe, an image that is predominantly blue, for example a tropical island. The bright blue sparkling ocean is lapping the seashore. Picture yourself sitting on the sand staring at the water as it glistens in the sun. Smell the fresh air, feel the sand between your toes, hear the lapping waves, the birds in the trees, taste the salty air. Concentrate on this image as you breathe in and out. Check for tension in your body. Are you feeling more relaxed?
- Once you feel a little more relaxed, think of an image that is predominantly green, for example a

pine forest. Walk through the trees, see the bright green pine needles, look up through the canopy, smell the pine, touch a branch and taste the fresh air. Keep belly breathing and stay with the image until you feel a little more relaxed.

- Go back to the image of the sea, then back to the pine forest, in your own time, changing your focus from one scenario to the other.
- Once you are feeling relaxed, visualize something orange. It can be as simple as an actual orange. Remember to belly breathe. Again, do the sensory recall, smell, taste, touch, feel, see, and even hear what noise it makes when you put it down. How heavy does it feel in your hand? Now open your eyes.

RELAXATION EXERCISES

Hand trace

This exercise will help you calm and focus your mind. Remember to use your belly breathing throughout.

- Place your left or your right hand in front of you, palm up.
- Use the index finger of your other hand to slowly trace a small clockwise circle in the palm of your upturned hand.
- Now trace a line from the centre of your palm, up over the base of the thumb and continue to trace around the outside of the thumb, around the index finger and then continue around the edge of all your fingers, finishing with tracing the small circle in the palm.
- Repeat on the other hand.

Animal breathing

We love this calming connection; it really is so simple, and our autistic children seem to benefit from it.

If you have a pet, they can be one of the best ways to proactively model calm and help your child to connect to calm breathing. Do not attempt this if your cat or dog is a little temperamental or unpredictable – if they are, this may not be the exercise for you and your child. This is to be done in Clear Time to begin with. Although this exercise needs to be embedded first, it can be a very effective 'go to' exercise for crunch moments.

- When your cat or dog is fast asleep, sit or lie next to them and breathe with your pet.
- Ask your child if they would like to play.
- Don't worry if they don't want to do it at first, just try it again at another time.

VISUALIZATION EXERCISE

Imagine if...

- Lie down. If the child feels safe to do so, ask them to close their eyes.
- Start with 'Imagine if...' then paint some verbal 'imagination pictures' for them. The imagination pictures should be peaceful and relatable.
- Use a low, slow tone and try to speak in a heartbeat rhythm; for example, use their special interest to paint the imagination pictures.
- 'Imagine if you were floating in the sky holding a pink heart balloon. The sun is shining, you look down and you are floating over your house.

You float over the house and what do you see in the garden? Little baby ladybirds and ants having a party. They are drinking juice and eating cake.'

- Or, 'Can you see Thomas? He's driving around the garden. Look, he's waving.'

As we have described before in this book, all our exercises are for you to personalize. You know your child better than anyone else, so 'lean in' to their passions. Your child may not like Thomas the Tank Engine or insects but there will be something that really engages them, so enter their world. Do this calmly and you will be connecting empathetically without even trying.

PROCESSING GAMES

Energy circle

This exercise works on many levels. The children are interacting and being physical, which taps into their sensory state. They are processing instructions and they are having fun.

- Ask the group to stand in a circle.
- Explain that each person will create an action and a sound, and check to see that everyone wants to play. Model some actions and sounds; for example, a jump and a snake hissing, a knee bend and a bird singing.
- Instruct everyone to focus on the centre of the circle. Check that everyone has an action and a sound. Group members help those who are finding it hard.
- One person starts with their action and sound, the

person to their left then repeats it. The action and sound are sent clockwise around the circle and when it gets back to the first person, they take a bow and everybody claps and says 'Bravo'.

- The person to the left of the first child then does their action and sound and sends it clockwise around the circle, etc. Continue with the next person and so on. If players don't want to play, they can just say 'Pass', or you can pass for them.

Guess the action

This exercise engages the imagination and helps develop concentration and cognitive dexterity. It also provides mime ideas for children who might find verbalizing difficult. The idea is that the child mimes the last thing that was said.

- Ask the group to sit in a circle.
- Enter the circle and mime an action, such as polishing windows, skipping with an imaginary skipping rope, washing your hands, or anything else you can think of.
- Tell the group that one of them must enter the circle and ask you, 'What are you doing?' You reply, 'Driving a car', or anything that doesn't look like the mime you were doing.
- You return to the sitting circle and the person who asked the question mimes driving a car.
- Someone else comes into the circle and asks, 'What are you doing?' The person replies, 'Swimming', or anything that doesn't look like driving a car.

- Continue for as long as the group is focused and enjoying themselves.

SEQUENCING AND IMAGINATION EXERCISE

The event

This exercise requires collaboration and communication and will help with developing relationships and practising interaction. It requires some preparation.

- Create about 16 event cards. On each card, write an event such as a wedding, a funeral, a party, an explosion, a dance, a swimming lesson – anything that the children might engage with.
- Put the cards face down.
- Allocate groups of three. Let each person in a group choose a card.
- Once all the groups have chosen cards, get the children to stand in a circle.
- Each group should tell the other groups what they have on their cards. Tell the groups that they must create a story using all the events. Give examples.
- Tell them they have ten minutes to rehearse their story.
- Show the performances.
- Applaud after each performance.

COLLABORATION EXERCISE

Creating stories together

The funnier the story the better, but try and encourage a balance between making sense and using imagination. In any game, be playful, non-judgemental, make mistakes yourself, be full of praise and finish before the child gets bored or agitated, which may show itself in unfocused or disruptive energy.

One-word story

This exercise can be played in the car, on a walk or sitting side by side.

- One person in the family or workshop starts by saying one word and the next person says another word. The object of the communication is to build a story word by word.
- You can play with two people or as many as you like. It is useful to give a demonstration to show your child how it will work. Show yourself getting it wrong and being silly too. To help keep order, the person who goes first is the person who decides when full stops or restarts can happen.
- After a few rounds, someone volunteers to recount the whole story as accurately as they can: *One-day-a-dog-ate-mushrooms-and-had-to-go-to-the-moon...*

One-sentence story

These are fun games, but they also model and encourage useful skills like listening, being flexible and using the imagination in a context. These games can be fun and bonding as well as useful opportunities to build communication skills and understanding of certain principles like turn-taking and listening. We suggest that fun is the priority.

- This is the same as the one-word story, but each person adds a sentence to the story.
- Play with two people or as many as you like.

These are just a few of our favourite exercises but there are many excellent books full of fun and educative games and exercises.

Chapter 14

Additional 3C
Pathway Exercises

'I've shared the exercises I've learned with my husband and friends, so they understand our child better.'

(Benita, parent)

These exercises are for you to explore once you are confident with the three steps of the 3C Pathway. Some of them appear earlier in the book, but if you are anything like us you will hate finding a good exercise when reading, and then wondering where it is when you leaf through the book later to find it.

As parents and carers, consider yourself the translator

or guide. You are the link to an unknown language for your child, the language of emotions, needs and wants. Through the 3C Pathway we can help them towards emotional literacy. Knowing how to ask for a drink is one thing, but knowing how to tell someone you love them, or that you are feeling sad or worried is also vital. Always remember the Connection step of the 3C Pathway never ends.

EVERYDAY CONNECTIONS

Joining

Spend moments in the day just being alongside your child involved in a passive activity yourself. Reading, listening to music, looking at a view, walking in silence. You must be clear of anxiety, distraction and expectation (Clear Time connections). Make sure you are calm, ideally not talking, and regulate your breathing. If they ask you what you are doing, just say, for example, 'I am just relaxing, having a rest.' You don't have to be close at first, just aim to be in the same room.

Subtle mirroring

Join in with their rhythms and movement *but* do this slowly. If the movement is giving them pleasure, show you are enjoying it too. Mirror their sounds but at a reduced level, slower and calmer. If using words, use slower, even rhythms and lower tones.

Heartbeat hug

Hug your child and softly tap a heartbeat on their back (some children love this, some don't – as with all the exercises it is not a one size fits all). Experiment with hugs or other ways of sharing the heartbeat rhythms. Tap on their arm or leg. Use a pillow, tap on a surface, beat a drum. Eventually, if it seems appropriate, share with your child the reason why you are doing heartbeat rhythms; for example, 'I feel calmer when I do this', 'I was feeling anxious, so I am doing this.' Remember, we are not 'doing to' or strategizing; we are modelling calm, leaning in and tuning in to their communications.

Conscious validation

Make unsolicited comments relating to your child's efforts, or appearance that do not require a response; for example: '*Great* shirt choice', 'Thanks for telling me you were upset at school – it helps me to help you', 'Thanks for being patient and waiting your turn to have a glass of water', 'Spending time with you is lovely.' Remember, keep it simple.

PROACTIVE CONNECTIONS

Movement mirroring

Encourage physical activity that you can do together where you can mirror your child's movements and sound. Try incorporating a heartbeat rhythm into the activity (this is often a good way of calming at the same time). Try jumping, throwing, trampolining, rolling, running, swaying – all done in a non-competitive, fun way where you are reacting and responding to their movements rather than leading. If they don't want to play, stop but still validate them: 'That was fun.'

To and fro mirroring

Introduce your own movements and encourage your child to copy, leading to reciprocal movements and sound. If they don't want to play, stop and return to you leading at another time. They may be overwhelmed or simply not in the mood.

Promoting their special interest

Make the first move to talk about your child's favourite thing, maybe buying a book or looking on the internet. Find out what's new, and maybe arrange a visit somewhere to extend their knowledge. Lean in to whatever they enjoy; even if you are not interested in, for example, computer gaming, try to lean in by saying, 'I love you, you love games, teach me please.'

CRUNCH CONNECTIONS

Side-beat-breath-low-slow

Be alongside, rather than face-to-face as this can feel threatening. Check into your heartbeat, your energy and rhythms, by putting your hand on your heart and beating 60 beats per minute.

Breathe in through your nose and out through your mouth, making sure that the out-breath is longer. If you do speak or make a sound, keep it to a low tone and keep it rhythmically slow.

EVERYDAY CALMING

Belly breaths – for you

This exercise is a good starting point for connecting with your breathing. Using your diaphragm (the muscle that is just beneath the ribs), try expanding the belly as you breathe in for three counts. Breathe out for six counts contracting your belly as you breathe out. You will feel your belly expand on the in-breath if you are doing this right. This deep breathing really helps relax your body and clear your anxious thoughts.

Trigger check

Become a detective and notice what things make your child anxious. Notice that anxiety for them can be a delayed response, so try to work out what has happened during the day. Don't comment on it, or ask why they are anxious, just try to work out if there are any recurring situations that could be triggering anxiety about the present situation or something that happened earlier.

PROACTIVE CALMING

Heartbeat massage

Put your left hand on your heart, put your right hand on top of your left hand, inhale deeply through your nose, filling your chest with air. Exhale through your mouth as you press on your heart. Try to empty the lungs and only inhale again, through the nose, when you really need to. Repeat approximately five times or until you feel more relaxed and centred.

CRUNCH CALMING

'You're safe.' 'I'm here.'

Keep repeating this in a heartbeat rhythm, in low and slow tones, but if your child starts to get more agitated, remember that you can 'say everything by saying nothing'. Simply stay alongside, gently tapping a heartbeat rhythm. Remember the story of Honey the spaniel's instinctive reaction in Chapter 1.

Pacing

When your child is running, run alongside them taking your pace down slowly. Don't try to change the pace too quickly and notice that your child will begin to slow down too. Try tapping a heartbeat rhythm on your thigh as you move. You are validating their self-regulation at the same time as bringing their energy down to a manageable level.

Beat to beat

If your child is hitting out, get a cushion and punch the cushion in a heartbeat rhythm. When they hit, you do a heartbeat 'beat/beat' between each of their hits. Slowly lessen your 'beat/beats' so that there is more and more space between your beat/beats on the cushion.

EVERYDAY COMMUNICATION

The story our bodies tell – a personal check-in

Consider when you ask, 'How was your day?', whose needs are you meeting in this transaction? Is it for the child's well-being or because you are desperate for a connection and validation? Questions are hard for autistic children and create anxiety, as many worry about giving the 'right' answer. Consider your mode and manner of communication. Consider that the sensory environment and your 'noise' and 'verbage', as we call it, are probably increasing the sensory load. Do some breathing or heartbeat work as you consider this.

Heartbeat rhythms

Use the heartbeat rhythm principle outlined in Chapter 12. Speak in a steady heartbeat rhythm, avoiding varied inflections and keeping your pace regular.

As we have discussed, *communication starts with reflection, not action*. Take the time to genuinely assess the situation, scenario and environment.

When we are in the moment, we may feel at times that we haven't got time for this reflection, but the minutes you take to reflect can save you hours later.

Passive non-verbal signs and cues

Communicate when you are alongside. This means your child can choose what they focus on, and they don't feel the pressure of negotiating eye contact. We also communicate with our face and body, but autistic children can find these cues difficult to read and so prefer less direct 'communication'. In any communication early on, let the child lead the conversation and finish when the child indicates they have had enough.

PROACTIVE COMMUNICATION

Things you can do together

Join them in whatever takes your child's interest or in their 'special interest'. If you are connecting calmly through shared communication about something that fuels their imagination, even if it holds no interest for you, or you can't see the sense in it, we encourage it. This is a great starting point. It is in these moments that they are communicating authentically and in relationship with another person, who will not judge, or 'move them on'. This has more value than just the verbal communication, and children often exhibit joy and relaxation when engaged in activities and conversations of their choosing. Your active listening and validation of their communication mode will show them you have 'seen them' and 'heard them', which is more powerful than you can imagine.

Conscious conversations – naming your emotions

When you feel something, let them know what it is, explain clearly why and how you feel it and where in your body you feel it. 'I am cross today because I got a parking ticket. I am cross with myself, because it was my fault, and I now will have to pay £60. I feel cross in my chest. It's tight and I want to cry a bit. If I cry, I will feel a bit better.'

You don't have to be an expert. You just simply explain what you feel, why you feel it, and what you can do about it. 'Sad heart' (point to your heart, make a sad face). 'I lost my purse. I want to cry' (point to your eyes). Explain, 'I feel better after crying.'

Alongside activities

Make an emotions diary, dictionary, scrapbook or poster. Do this with your child as an activity. Use pictures cut from magazines, draw emoji faces, use colour coding for emotions; for example, ask them what colour is an angry colour, then use that colour to draw something.

Possible or probable

Our children often find it hard to deal with uncertainty or situations they can't control. Saying 'Don't worry, it will be okay' not only invalidates their anxiety but will probably be met with an escalation in anxiety. Consider the question 'Will the spider bite me?'. You could answer, 'It's possible, but do you think it probably will? Do you know anyone who has been bitten by a spider?' If they say yes, connect with them by saying, 'Let's do some research and see how probable it is that spiders bite people.' Whatever the worry is, don't shut it down. Explore the probability by starting with 'It's possible, but...' This strategy systematically de-escalates the worry and gives them a structured answer.

The story of emotions

Take key emotions and break them down. What do we call them? Why do they manifest? Where do people feel them in their body? How do people manage them? As an example, say, 'When I am nervous, I have a tickly tummy.' Point at your tummy as you say it.

Emotional exploration

Use puppets and toys to explore emotional range and emotional confusion. Use two toys – one may be shouting to a friend to get their attention but they are not cross. The toy may look sad, but they are just tired because they have been working hard. You can do this for your own expressions too: 'When I use a loud voice, I am not always cross – sometimes I am excited.'

Emotion ladder

Draw an image that indicates things going up and explain how emotions can go up and come down. Show your emotions on the ladder first, then create a system of ladders for your child's emotions, either to refer to regularly in everyday situations or to use in challenging situations: 'Today we are going to the shops to get new shoes.' Point to the ladder with different emotions and levels on it and say, 'Point to how you feel about that.' 'I notice that you seem worried about school – can you point to the step on the ladder that tells me how high your anxiety level is today?'

Mood board

Using a dry-wipe board, draw or stick on symbols representing different emotions and allow your child to indicate with a marker pen how they feel today. Validate your child whenever they communicate with you: just a simple 'Thanks for letting me know. You did really well in explaining what you feel.'

I feel – I need

Create two lists, one containing the feelings that your child understands and then a second list alongside it of potential needs and things they may want to do in relation to the emotion, or things that need to happen to make them feel okay. This list can expand over time and the child can direct you to what they need even when they can't find the words.

Feelings	Needs
I am sad	I need to swing
I am cross	I need you to go away
I am happy	I need to jump
I am thirsty	I need my juice bottle
I am agitated	I need to shout

Shared signs

Create and use shared signs. It doesn't matter what the signs are when you have a common understanding, a private language even, between you. For older children, things like thumbs up, thumbs down are a good step up from pictures to let you know what they want in response to questions you ask. Texting is also a useful tool. Parents often tell us they use text emojis even when they are sitting next to their child.

Heartbeat 'parcels of communication'

Try using calm, short sentences with no rising inflections. 'Hi there. Come in, sit yourself down. Lovely to see you, really glad you came.' This is a warm, simple greeting, but what if, instead, you used a heartbeat rhythm, 'Come in', and gestured to the chair, 'Sit down', and you sit down alongside your child and without looking at them conclude with 'I'm glad you're here.' Practise this a few times until it feels more natural.

Now try saying the instructions again and internalize the heartbeat by saying to yourself 'and one, and two'. It takes some practice but if your child is finding it hard to access instructions, it is worth trying heartbeat 'parcels of communication'.

Modelling and sharing

When your child is not in distress, talk to them about the exercises. Tell them that the exercises help you to de-stress/make you calm down/help you feel happy. Keep modelling, not strategizing! You can use a fitness tracker to help you explain by running on the spot and checking your pulse afterwards, then saying that sometimes your heart rate is high when you feel anxious.

CRUNCH COMMUNICATION

Say everything by saying nothing

The best communication from you is often non-verbal. You should be saying non-verbally, 'You are safe', 'I am close' and 'I understand why you are feeling overwhelmed.' When you do speak, use as few words as possible: 'I hear you', 'I see you', 'I hear what you are saying.'

After a meltdown

Allow the child to communicate about the meltdown in any way and whenever they are ready. This will help them, and you, become more familiar with the meltdown, the triggers and their needs. They may not want to discuss it until several hours later. Do not push the communication.

Help them to use analogies; for example, 'It felt like a big beast in my chest' or 'It felt like all the lights went out.' Draw a picture of how it felt, even a scribble or colouring a page will help. Art therapists call this 'flow', because by using your body, the movement of the hand connects your body and mind. Give the feeling a name; for example, 'black tar', 'jabbing knives', or make up words, such as 'flump' or 'smaaaaah'.

These are all ways of communicating feelings to validate the child by helping them to understand, and helping others to understand, their differences.

Conclusions

In reading this book, you have demonstrated care and curiosity for the child or young person you love, live with, work with or care for. None of us can expect to always 'get it right' but by continually remaining open to the emotional, physical and verbal cues our children give us, we can not only become their best advocate, but also support their development clear of our own expectations, anxiety and distractions. By using Act for Autism's relational approach, the 3C Pathway, we not only validate our children at a visceral level, but also give them the freedom to be their best self. Keeping vigilant in a calm, caring and curious mode will help them, and you, to an ultimate acceptance of your relationship. It will also assist your relationships and communications with your child and their wider circle of friends, family and the community.

References

Addabbo, M., Longhi, E., Marchis, I.C., Tagliabue, P. and Turat, C. (2018) 'Dynamic facial expressions of emotions are discriminated at birth.' *PLoS One, 13*(3) e0193868.

Caldwell, P. (2014) *The Anger Box*. Hove, East Sussex: Pavilion Publishing and Media Ltd.

Fletcher-Watson, S. and Happé, F. (2019) *Autism, A New Introduction to Psychological Theory and Current Debate*. Abingdon, Oxfordshire: Routledge.

Grandin, T. (2013) *The Autistic Brain*. Boston, MA: Houghton Mifflin Harcourt Publishing Company.

Higashida, N. (2007) *The Reason I Jump*. London: Sceptre, Hodder and Stoughton.

Reynolds, D. and Reason, M. (2012) *Kinesthetic Empathy in Creative and Cultural Practices*. Bristol: Intellect.

The New York Times (2014) 'Study finds that brains with autism fail to trim synapses as they develop.' 21 August.

Index

**Having Fun with Feelings on
the Autism Spectrum**
A CBT Activity Book for Kids
Age 4–8
*Michelle Garnett, Tony Attwood,
Louise Ford, Stefanie Runham
and Julia Cook*

£9.99 I $13.95 I PB I 96PP
I ISBN 978 1 78775 327 3 I
eISBN 978 1 78775 328 0

This activity book is designed to be used by children on the autism spectrum aged 4–8. The workbook introduces them to 6 'feelings' characters who help them to recognize and express different emotions to reduce anxiety. It is intended to be used with the accompanying guidebook, *10 Steps to Reducing Your Child's Anxiety on the Autism Spectrum*.

10 Steps to Reducing Your Child's Anxiety on the Autism Spectrum
The CBT-Based 'Fun with Feelings' Parent Manual
Michelle Garnett, Tony Attwood, Louise Ford, Stefanie Runham and Julia Cook

£14.99 I $24.95 I PB I 256PP
I ISBN 978 1 78775 325 9 I
eISBN 978 1 78775 326 6

This manual is designed to help parents of children on the autism spectrum aged 4–8 support their children with emotional regulation to decrease anxiety. This CBT-based programme is structured around 10 stages and is intended to be used with the activity book *Having Fun with Feelings on the Autism Spectrum*.

Life Will Never Be Dull
The Little Book of Autism
Adventures
Deborah Brownson MBE
Illustrated by Michelle Rebello-Tindall

£9.99 | $16.95 | HB | 80PP
| ISBN 978 1 78775 322 8 |
eISBN 978 1 78775 323 5

'A sense of humour definitely helps, as will sleep, and did I mention wine...?'

This delightful book is a light-hearted, playful and sincere look at life with an autistic child. Humorous illustrations depict those unique moments that every autistic child's family will recognize, and gently remind the reader to take care of themselves and appreciate the many wonderful experiences of being a mother, father, brother or sister to an autistic person.

Fifteen Things They Forgot to Tell You About Autism
The Stuff That Transformed My Life as an Autism Parent
Debby Elley

£12.99 I $19.95 I PB I 224PP
I ISBN 978 1 78592 438 5 I
eISBN 978 1 78450 810 4

What if the things people need to know about autism is not the information they're getting? Combining myth-busting advice with personal experience, this book from the mother of autistic twins shares simple strategies to build children's confidence, communication and independence.

From sharing the joy of yodelling around shops at the weekend, to finding creative ways to communicate with both her verbal and her non-verbal sons, Debby Elley gives practical and fun tips for everyday living and shows that being autistic is just another way of being. Both witty and candid, the book discusses labels, meltdowns, acceptance, happiness and much more.